THE LINCOLN STORY

THE LINCOLN STORY

The Postwar Years

Thomas E. Bonsall

STANFORD GENERAL BOOKS
An Imprint of Stanford University Press
Stanford, California 2004

Stanford University Press
Stanford, California

Printed in the United States of America
on acid-free, archival-quality paper.

Library of Congress Cataloging-in-Publication Data

Bonsall, Thomas E.
The Lincoln story : the postwar years / Thomas E. Bonsall.
p. cm.
Includes index.
ISBN 0-8047-4941-8 (alk. paper)
1. Lincoln automobile—History. 2. Lincoln Motor Company—(Detroit, Mich.)—History. I. Title.
TL215.L5 B6623 2003
629.222'2—dc21 2003017121

Original Printing 2003

Last figure below indicates year of this printing:
12 11 10 09 08 07 06 05 04 03

Designed by James P. Brommer
Typeset in 11/15 Garamond

Contents

Acknowledgments

The author is indebted to numerous individuals and organizations who have assisted the research that went into this book. This list includes Ed Gorman, Lincoln-Mercury's public relations manager when my original Lincoln research was undertaken in 1980. He died prior to the completion of that research, but this book benefits mightily from his long-ago support. James Olson, then with Lincoln-Mercury Division and now with Toyota, also contributed. Richard Stout, a former member of the product planning staff at the Lincoln-Mercury Division and later at Packard and still later back at Lincoln-Mercury Division again, submitted to several invaluable interviews. Numerous people within Ford Motor Company assisted in ways large and small through the years from various departments, including Lincoln-Mercury Division, the Design Center, the Industrial Archives, and Photomedia.

THE LINCOLN STORY

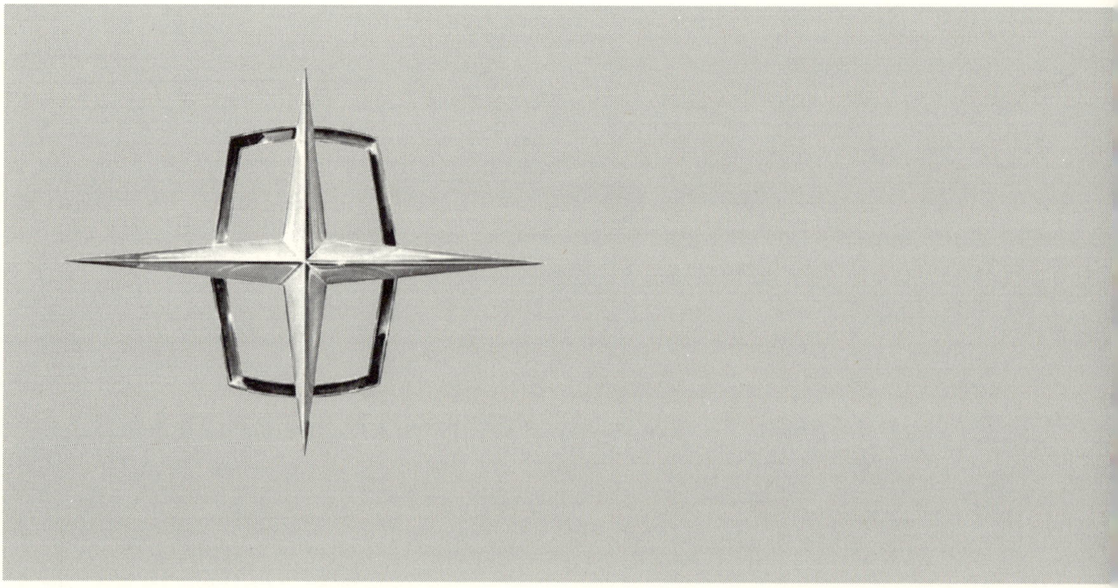

Henry Ford, *standing left*, and Henry Leland at the purchase of the Lincoln Motor Car Company by Ford in February, 1922. The sons are seated: Edsel Ford, *left*, and Wilfred Leland.

Introduction

LINCOLN CELEBRATED its eightieth anniversary in 2001, and February 4, 2002 marked the eightieth anniversary of the purchase of the Lincoln Motor Car Company by Ford. The seventieth and seventy-fifth anniversaries had been marked by commemorative books and special events, but the eightieth was allowed to pass unnoticed. It's not that there was nothing to celebrate; Lincoln has been selling very well of late. The problem is that during the preceding decade Ford Motor Company had came to own so many luxury brands—Aston Martin, Jaguar, Volvo and Land Rover—that it suddenly found itself tripping over its own toes and badly in need of a way to organize the mess.

Lincoln had always been Ford's luxury flagship. Now the company had five luxury brands, and Lincoln's mission—along with its anniversary—got lost in the shuffle. To remedy this situation, they might start by studying Lincoln's post-World War II history. That subject is the reason for this volume. And an honorable story it is, too.

Lincoln's heritage is, in fact, as rich as that of any car built anywhere in the world, and far more impressive than all but a few. The Lincoln Continental of 1940, for example, was one of the first cars to be universally recognized by classic car cognoscenti. Never a mere used car, it went directly from current production status to being a much sought-after collectible, a record that few classics have ever matched. The list of Lincoln-built cars in the postwar era certified with classic or comparable "milestone" status by various sanctioning bodies is likewise lengthy. And, of course, generations of Americans have known it as the Car of Presidents; since the days of Franklin Roosevelt, the White House has exhibited a marked preference for Lincolns.

Clearly, Lincoln has won a large measure of well-deserved respect. Even so, it remains curiously underrated. For example, only one truly comprehensive Lincoln history has ever been published—and it is long out of print. By contrast, one could load a good-sized bookshelf to the point of structural failure with books on other luxury marques that have been built through the years—only a bare handful of which have survived the test of time, and most of them treasured mainly for their rarity, their overwrought excesses, or their glorious impracticality.

Why is this so? Part of it is the inverse value we tend to place on volume. The more plentiful an item is, the less we appreciate it and vice versa. Nowhere is this more true than with collector cars. Although Lincoln was rarely until recently a sales leader in the luxury field, it built far too many cars to compete for cachet with certain smaller foreign brands whose names are uttered in hushed tones by aficionados.

Lincoln also suffers as a result of our distorted cultural bias toward things American. When it comes to Mass Culture, we think—unreasonably—that no one else in the world can hold a candle to us. When it comes to quality (from luxury goods to the fine arts) it is just the reverse. We automatically grant special status to things foreign, while reflexively denigrating our own achievements or, perhaps worse, ignoring them altogether. It has long been a cliche in the arts, for example, that all-too-often an American artist (performer, painter, whatever) cannot gain acceptance in America until he or she has established a name abroad; only when Europeans give their stamp of approval will we readily give our native sons and daughters a fair hearing. Every educated American knows of Picasso, but how many could name a 20th Century American painter?

It is no different with high-quality automobiles. If it is built in the Black Forest by elves, it is accorded an instant respect an American car maker has to struggle for years to attain. In the area of our finer accomplishments, people around the world tend to have a better appreciation for us than we do ourselves. (After all, Picasso drove a Lincoln.) One wonders what sort of popular mythology would have grown up around Lincoln—and how much more Ford could charge—if it had an unpronounceable foreign name and came from over there.

Make no mistake about it, few cars built anywhere in the world during the past six decades have surpassed Lincoln in either the richness of its heritage or the excellence of its products. The cars have been unfailingly interesting, frequently magnificent and—in several instances—quite literally legends in their own time.

What is really striking about Lincoln's postwar development, though, is how haphazard it was. Unlike Cadillac, which had a successful formula it relentlessly pursued during good times and bad—except, significantly, during the 1980s when it faltered disastrously—Lincoln has not had a well-thought out, consistent mission or theme. Instead, the brand has been sent hither and yon in search of the magic formula that would transform it into America's premier luxury car.

Each of the postwar cars designed in the first two decades after the end of World War II, for example, were victims of this lack of focus. The 1949–51, 1952–55, 1956–57, 1958–60, and 1961–65 series cars were so lacking in continuity they could have been built by five different car companies. The 1949–51 series was tastefully designed by E. T. Gregorie, but the standard Lincoln models were originally intended as replacements for the prewar Ford. The 1952–55 series was dramatically recast by Ford's chief engineer, Earle MacPherson, in a smaller, more roadworthy package inspired by GM's Oldsmobile. It was a terrific road car, but no amount of fancy interior trim could make it fully competitive with contemporary Cadillacs in the minds of luxury car buyers. Lincoln-Mercury Division finally got the longer, lower, wider car it wanted with the 1956–57 series, but it was short-lived—again by edict from MacPherson who ordered the division to switch to unibody construction for 1958. The result was a styling and engineering failure that nearly killed the brand. Rescue came in the form of the "slab-sided" 1961–65 range—a car originally designed as a Thunderbird.

With the 1961 Continental and the Mark III in 1969, Lincoln at last seemed to stumble upon a winning formula—a tasteful sedan range balanced by a garish personal luxury coupe—and Lincoln sales rose steadily throughout the 1960s and 1970s. Unfortunately, the fuel crises of the 1970s turned these types of cars into dinosaurs and Ford's attempts to replace them met with one failure after another. Consider the history of the past quarter century. Lincoln has had thirteen major new product launches: Versaille (1977), Town Car and Mark VI (1980), Continental (1982), Mark VII (1984), Continental (1988), Town Car (1990), Mark VIII (1993), Continental (1995), Navigator (1998), Town Car (1998), and LS (2000), Blackwood (2001), and Aviator (2003). Of these, only four were major successes, two were middling, six were outright failures—and the jury is still out on one.

The reason for this checkered history has to do with the corporate structure of Ford Motor Company. Back in 1922, when Henry and Edsel Ford bought Lincoln, it was a self-contained automobile manufacturer with every function required to build cars, including engineering and manufacturing. By the end of World War II, Lincoln as a corporate entity had for all practical purposes ceased to exist. The creation of Lincoln-Mercury Division in 1947 made it official, for Lincoln-Mercury was a sales and marketing organization with virtually no direct control over design, engineering or manufacturing. That essentially remains the case today.

Cadillac, in contrast, remained a self-contained car company with a fair degree of autonomy within the General Motors system even after its acquisition in 1910, including design, engineering and manufacturing. The GM reorganization in 1984 altered this dramatically in the direction of the Ford Motor Company model, but Cadillac regained significant control over its engineering and manufacturing in 1987, and remains to this day the only automotive operating division at GM with any real autonomy at all. (Saturn, which also maintains some autonomy, is technically a wholly-owned GM subsidiary.)

As a result, it has been far easier for Cadillac to stay, as the politicians would put it, "on message" from decade to decade, while the Lincoln brand has flailed all over the map. Even as this is written—sixty years after the death of Lincoln's patron, Edsel Ford—Ford officials are still musing publicly about trying to define Lincoln's mission!

So how did Lincoln manage to come through the last few years in seemingly better shape than archrival Cadillac—and even in recent years achieve parity in sales? Simple. As bad as things were at Lincoln-Mercury in the 1980s, Cadillac did even worse. Even so, it wasn't the various Lincoln car lines that propelled the brand to its startling sales victory over Cadillac in 1998, it was the Navigator sport-utility truck.

All is not well, though. Lincoln passenger car sales have softened in recent times, as has the large sport-utility vehicle market. Worse, Cadillac again has a clear-cut mission upon which it is focused. Some industry observers are doubtful that this mission—which is known as "Art and Science"—will work miracles, but at least it is something. To paraphrase an old cliché, a second-rate mission given first-rate execution will always beat a first-rate mission given second-rate execution. For the time being, Lincoln has no clearly defined mission at all other than to keep doing what it has been doing and hope for the best.

That may not be enough in the face of a rapidly changing market. As recently as 1990, Lincoln and Cadillac dominated American luxury sales. Then the Baby-Boomers began to constitute an increasing percentage of luxury vehicle buyers, and they, in turn, will be followed in due course by the Gen Xers. Those groups are indifferent—if not hostile—to traditional American concepts of luxury. This has sparked a tremendous boom in foreign and Japanese luxury brands—BMW, Mercedes-Benz, Lexus, etc.—to say nothing of Ford's own brands, such as Volvo and Jaguar. So Lincoln had won its seventy-eight-year-old battle with Cadillac only to find the rules of the game had changed.

A couple of comments are in order on the way in which this book has been put together. Since the intended audience includes enthusiasts, there is significant attention paid to product coverage. And since it has been the product cycles that have driven the Lincoln story since the end of World War II, the chapters have been arranged to conform to those cycles with, as nearly as possible, each told as if it were a self-contained story. The model proliferation in recent decades would, on the surface, seem a complicating factor. With all those cars (and now trucks) being built on different platforms, one would think that covering the products would become more and more difficult and require more and more space. Yet, this factor has been more than offset by Ford Motor Company's approach to vehicle development since 1980.

When Detroit realized it had a major quality problem, Ford was the first automaker to achieve notable results. One way it accomplished this was to ruthlessly develop new products before initial launch to make sure they were as nearly perfect as possible in every way, and then leave them more-or-less unchanged throughout their life cycles. Thus, a 1992 Mark VII was, except for detail refinements needed along the way, remarkably close to the first model in the series back at the launch in 1984. So while there are more platforms involved today than there were in the 1950s and 1960s, there were far more changes made from year to year back then than there are today.

At any rate, the next few years promise to be interesting ones for Lincoln. If we cannot predict the future, we can at least try to understand the past. That is what this book is about.

CHAPTER ONE

A pair of 1946 Lincolns. *Top*, a Continental; *bottom*, a convertible.

Edsel's Legacy, Part One: 1946–48

THE POSTWAR STORY for every American luxury brand car can be dated from the fall of 1935. That was when Cadillac and Lincoln announced completely new lines of cars built as no products wearing those nameplates ever had been. They joined an entirely new product from Packard that had arrived a few months before. To understand the im-portance of these models, a little history is in order.

The Great Depression prompted fundamental changes in how industrial America acted. Among the luxury car manufacturers, all came to more-or-less the conclusion that they needed more volume to survive and that moving down in price seemed to be the only way to get it.

Unfortunately, the traditional way of manufacturing luxury cars was so inefficient it made building less expensive cars a practical impossibility. The Lincoln plant at the corner of Warren and Livernois in Detroit was competitive by luxury producer standards, but it was practically Medieval compared to the state-of-the-art Ford production a few miles away at the Rouge plant.

The difference between the way in which the manufacturers behaved in the Ford class as compared to the Lincoln-Packard-Cadillac class cannot be overstressed, for it is central to an understanding of the agony all luxury car builders went through as they tried (and, in most cases, failed) to come to grips with the economic calamity that faced them. The Ford car had to be built to a price and, in order to render it profitable at that low level, expenses had to be ferociously monitored. The retail price was dictated by the demands of the marketplace, and no manufacturer of low-priced cars could charge even $25 more than the market dictated without running the risk of disaster. In other words, the manufacturer of low-priced cars could not cover its inefficiencies by arbitrarily raising prices to the consumer or by cheapening the product. That left only one solution: manufacturing costs had to be ruthlessly controlled.

Before the stock market crashed in October, 1929, the luxury market had been a different world. There, a difference in retail price of $25, or $50, or

Posed at the 1932 Indianapolis 500. *Left to right,* Eddie Rickenbacker, Henry, Edsel (seated at the wheel of a Lincoln KB-Series), Harvey Firestone, Jr., Henry II, Benson, and Harvey Firestone, Sr.

even a couple of hundred dollars had been meaningless. While it would be unfair to state that Lincolns in the 1920s had been built without any thought to their costs, the Lincoln plant was pretty much run according to a sort of cost-plus pricing system. In other words, whatever a Lincoln cost, something more was added for profit and that was the price quoted to the customer.

The approach worked well enough for many years because there was sufficient demand for damn-the-cost luxury rigs to support a practice that would have been lethal in the Ford class. The Depression brought the easy times to a crashing halt, though, and only when the luxury manufacturers, one by one, tried to build cars to a price did they come to grips with the dismal fact that they really didn't know how.

By 1932, all American luxury car manufacturers were awash in red ink. As a consequence, Franklin, Marmon, Pierce-Arrow, and Stutz were all either in receivership or soon to be. Peerless had already quit the field entirely, although the company survived. Lincoln, Packard and Cadillac survived only because they had powerful companies behind them ready to absorb their losses. Even so, the game would end sooner or later if something drastic weren't done to boost sales.

Packard had pointed the right direction with its moderately priced Light Eight series of 1932. The Light Eight had also come close to putting Packard out of business because it wasn't until it was in production that the company realized how ill-equipped it was to build cars to a price. So in order to follow the new direction, Packard would have to learn how to build cars with a revolutionary level of efficiency, as would Cadillac and Lincoln. The first result of this new way of thinking and doing was the hugely successful Packard One-Twenty. It had been introduced as a 1935 model. Now, the similar 1936 Cadillac Series Sixty and the Lincoln-Zephyr had also arrived—and Lincoln would never be the same. The traditional Lincolns—represented by the massive K-Series behemoths—were doomed. It was the Zephyr that pointed to Lincoln's future. Who would have thought such an outcome possible twenty years earlier when Henry Leland left General Motors to found the Lincoln Motor Company?

The Lincoln story began with Henry Leland, one of the unsung heroes of the early American auto industry. He was instrumental in the founding of Cadillac in 1902. Two decades later, after leaving General Motors, he founded the Lincoln Motor Car Company, named for his hero, Abraham Lincoln. That was in 1921, which turned out to be a Depression year and soon Lincoln was on the ropes, despite the engineering excellence of the original L-Series model. Henry and Edsel Ford came to the rescue with a buy-out offer and on February 4, 1922, Lincoln became part of the Ford empire.

Henry Ford received a tremendous amount of favorable free publicity for what was perceived as his good Samaritan deed. It was not, however, a marriage made in heaven. The Lelands were under the impression that they were going to continue to run Lincoln with almost complete autonomy under Ford ownership. Frictions were inevitable and, by June 13th, the Lelands were gone for good. Henry and his son, Wilfred Leland, who had been president and vice-president, respectively, were replaced by Edsel (formerly second vice-president) and Ernest C. Kanzler, Edsel's brother-in-law.

There is one fact about which even the Lelands must have agreed with the Fords: Lincoln quality remained high. In fact, if styling is taken into account, the Ford-built Lincolns were soon superior.

1936 Lincoln-Zephyr.

Edsel Ford was just the man Lincoln needed. The Lelands had provided the best chassis that they knew how to build, and now Edsel was determined to clothe it with coachwork of equal quality. There was a real synergy at work between the engineering genius of the Lelands and the innate aesthetic brilliance of Edsel. The automobile had matured from being a form of mere transportation to being a means of realizing ever escalating standards of luxury, comfort and beauty. The transition was beyond the grasp of the Lelands and the elder Ford, but Edsel understood the challenge. Lincoln's survival depended on it.

The most urgent need was to upgrade Lincoln coachwork to match the Leland engineering. It was a task Edsel approached with relish. His method was to solicit designs from the leading coachbuilders of the day, LeBaron, Locke, Judkins, Fleetwood (before it was swallowed up by GM), Brunn, Dietrich, Murray, and so on, and then order selected designs in lots of 50 or 100 or more. In this fashion, Edsel was able to offer the highest quality designs at prices far below what would have been charged for one-offs.

Toward the end of the decade, the L-Series Lincolns were moving toward the end of their life cycle, as well. Why Edsel moved backward in the alphabet in search of a designation for his next Lincoln is unknown. Perhaps this first Ford-designed Lincoln series was supposed to recall the last luxury car built by Ford—the Ford Model K of 1906. In any case, the 1931 Lincoln K was, by all accounts, a splendid machine and a worthy successor to the Leland-designed L. In fact, the KB series (powered by a 12-cylinder version of the Leland fork-and-blade V8) produced in 1932 and 1933 is regarded by more than a few classic car experts as the finest classic of all time from any manufacturer. Still, even that was not enough to overcome the financial calamity that had overtaken the nation during the Great Depression of the 1930s. Nothing seemed to work in a market that was vanishing day-by-day. The 1939 model was the end of the line for the K-Series.

Thanks to the foresight of Edsel Ford, the medium-priced Lincoln-Zephyr remained to carry on the name. Conceived in 1932 and introduced in 1936, the Zephyr sold well by Lincoln standards and succeeded in its primary mis-

1939 Lincoln Continental prototype.

sion of saving the brand from extinction. It was noted for both its streamlined styling—the first completely successful example in a mass production American car—and for its troublesome V12 engine. The latter was a stretched version of the Ford V8, and was in no way related to the celebrated K-Series V12.

The Zephyr was designed throughout under Edsel Ford's supervision, however. As a consequence, it did not receive the degree of engineering development a Ford would have had and the chassis—especially the engine—suffered for it. Many of the V12's problems were never adequately addressed during the ten model years of production and, in sum, the engine was not well regarded.

Perhaps the Zephyr's greatest aesthetic achievement was serving as the platform for the first one-off Continental in 1939. The original idea was to create a custom for Edsel's personal use with no plans to put it into volume production. The project began in September, 1938, when Edsel returned from Europe with ideas for a convertible coupe to be built with distinctively European lines. Moreover, it had to be built in time for his Florida vacation that winter. Edsel's first thought was to use the Ford chassis, or possibly that of the new Mercury. E. T. "Bob" Gregorie, chief of the styling studio, suggested the Zephyr.

1946 factory shot.

That decided, the details were all executed to Edsel's specifications using of as many off-the-shelf Zephyr parts as practical, although many were sectioned and cut-down, or lengthened. The car was completed in February, 1939, and shipped to Florida, where Edsel was vacationing. Edsel was enthusiastic. More to the point, Edsel's friends in Hobe Sound and Palm Beach—a circle which included much of the cream of the social register—were enthusiastic, too, and placed orders for upwards of two hundred copies should Edsel decided to put the Continental into production. He did.

With comparatively minor changes to make it suitable for volume manufacture, the Continental was officially announced to the public on October 2, 1939. The rest, as they say, is history. The Continental was beloved from the start and remained in production until 1948. It became an instant classic as soon as the last one rolled from the line.

The Zephyr also served as the platform for the successor to the K-Series: the Custom. Edsel was determined to have a big Lincoln in the catalog and so a stretched version of the Zephyr was developed. Produced in 1941 and 1942, the Lincoln Custom was a suitably large and impressive car—the White House acquired one for President Roosevelt's use—and it, together with the Continental, successfully sustained the Lincoln presence in the luxury field.

Normal development work on Ford, Mercury and Lincoln lines was proceeding when the United States entered the war in December, 1941. New Fords and Mercurys were planned for the 1943 model year as per their usual two year cycle. The Zephyr, with its unibody construction and lower production volume, was on a much longer cycle. The original Zephyr body had been new in 1936, then revised in 1938. The second Zephyr body was new for 1940 and revised for 1942. It seemed logical, therefore, to expect another new body for 1944, or certainly for 1945. A new Zephyr was, in fact, laid down as early as 1941 with well developed clays in existence by September of that year. These clays all give testimony to the love affair E. T. Gregorie and Edsel Ford were having with fastback styling. Unfortunately, this work ground almost completely to a halt with the American declaration of war as the entire industry was shifted to war assignments.

An even more devastating blow fell in May, 1943, with the death of Edsel Ford. Lincoln had lost its great patron, its de facto chief designer, and its great conceptual genius all at once. Worse, Ford Motor Company was undergoing a messy battle between the old guard, led by Henry Ford's personnel chief Harry Bennett, and the progressive forces, led by Edsel's eldest son, Henry Ford II. In September, 1945, the progressives won control just in time for resumption of peacetime automobile production.

1947 Continental.

When the war came to an end, the public had been without new cars to buy for almost four years. This tremendous pent-up demand prompted the greatest seller's market in the history of the industry, and it took almost eight years for the market to return to normal. In the meantime, the manufacturers had a field day, at least in terms of supply and demand. Especially in the early post-World War II period, almost anything that moved could be sold. Anticipating this, the manufacturers at first concentrated on producing only mildly refined versions of their 1942 models. This was certainly true in Lincoln's case. The biggest change was on the price list: prices were up by an average of 34 percent and would go even higher during the next few years.

Going into the postwar period, the Lincoln was a car with a "name," but without a well-defined identity. The L and K Lincolns had been limited run cars of extreme quality and price. The Zephyr had continued the Lincoln name into the 1940s after the death of the K, but despite the deletion of the "Zephyr" designation after the war and the use of the slogan "Nothing Could Be Finer," it remained a distinctly middle class car of somewhat checkered reputation. The Zephyr spin-offs, the Continental and the Custom, did valuable service in keeping the Lincoln name alive as a luxury car producer.

In August, 1945, the process of reconversion to peacetime automobile production began at the Lincoln plant, and, on September 13th, the first 1946 Lincoln rolled from the line. The postwar line consisted of Lincolns and Lincoln Continentals. Both Customs and the Zephyr three-passenger coupe were dropped. The Custom series had existed because Edsel Ford wanted it to. When he died, it died. The Continental, another one of his favorites was returned to the line-up but was clearly living on borrowed time.

There was no new sheet metal in the 1946 Lincolns. Styling alterations were limited to the grille and ornamental trim. The grille was a massive, diecast, egg crate design. Also new were hood ornaments, hood side moldings, hub caps and bumper guards. Postwar interiors were little changed.

Mechanical differences were, likewise, of a minor order, and the two significant ones were done in mid-year. Engine bore was reduced to 27/8 inches. This returned the engine to its 1941 displacement. Also in mid-run, a new oil pump was added with a revised intake screen and greater capacity.

Production levels were depressed for all makes during the unusual 1946 model year. Strikes and materials shortages hounded the industry without letup and none of the manufacturers reached their optimistic production goals. Lincoln production totaled 16,645 units.

Changes in the 1947 Lincoln and Continental models were mostly limited to extremely minor styling tweaks. Underneath, the compression ratio of the engine was increased to 7.2 to 1, and this upped the horsepower to 125. There were no meaningful changes to the interior.

All the 1946 models were continued over for 1947, and total production rose a bit to 21,460. In November, 1947, the 1948 models officially entered production. Aside from a few detail modifications to the trim, they were unchanged from the 1947 models. Only 7,769 were built before the model run ended with the unusually early announcement of the all-new 1949s. With the exception of a few Continentals, 1948 model production ended on January 19, 1948.

A corporate development of importance occurred toward the end of the model run: In October, the Lincoln-Mercury Division was created and Lincoln-Mercury dealerships blossomed across the land. In addition, the upcoming merging of Mercury and Lincoln bodies for the 1949 model year was seen as a significant merging of conceptual and corporate identities. The Mercury was henceforth to be regarded as a "baby" Lincoln, rather than as a gussied up Ford. Clearly things were happening at Lincoln-Mercury.

CHAPTER TWO

1949 Cosmopolitan.

Edsel's Legacy, Part Two: 1949–51

ON OCTOBER 22, 1946, Thomas W. Skinner was named to head the Lincoln Motor company. Skinner's was but one of dozen of key appointments made at the behest of the young president, Henry II, as the venerable Ford Motor Company was reorganized from top to bottom. The proposed 1949 product line was designed to be substantially altered as a result of this reorganization.

The development of the 1949-series Lincolns had begun as early as the summer of 1941, but was cut short by the war and did not resume until the war's end approached. E. T. Gregorie had left the company in the aftermath of Edsel Ford's death in 1943, but returned within the year as chief designer of the 1949 postwar Ford, Mercury and Lincoln lines. His staff then included Thomas L. Hibbard, who had taken over his duties during his absence from the company, Martin Regitko, who had helped design the first Continental, and, within a few months, Hermann C. Brunn, the former coachbuilder. This team had the new company products well in hand by the summer of 1945.

Then all hell broke loose. Ernest R. Breech, whom Henry II had recruited as vice-president and chief operating officer in 1946, and his new chief engineer, Harold T. Youngren, did not like the proposed 1949 Ford. They thought it much too heavy and Henry II concurred. This prompted a bizarre situation of musical chairs as all of the proposed car lines were knocked up one notch: the proposed Ford became the Mercury and the smaller Lincoln, the proposed smaller Lincoln became the top-of-the-line Lincoln Cosmopolitan, and the proposed top-of-the-line Lincoln was scrapped. If nothing else, it made a mess of Lincoln's carefully thought-out product program. Since there was no longer a Ford, a design competition for a new one was held between Gregorie and outside consultant George Walker. When the Walker proposal won a "blind" selection, Gregorie resigned again.

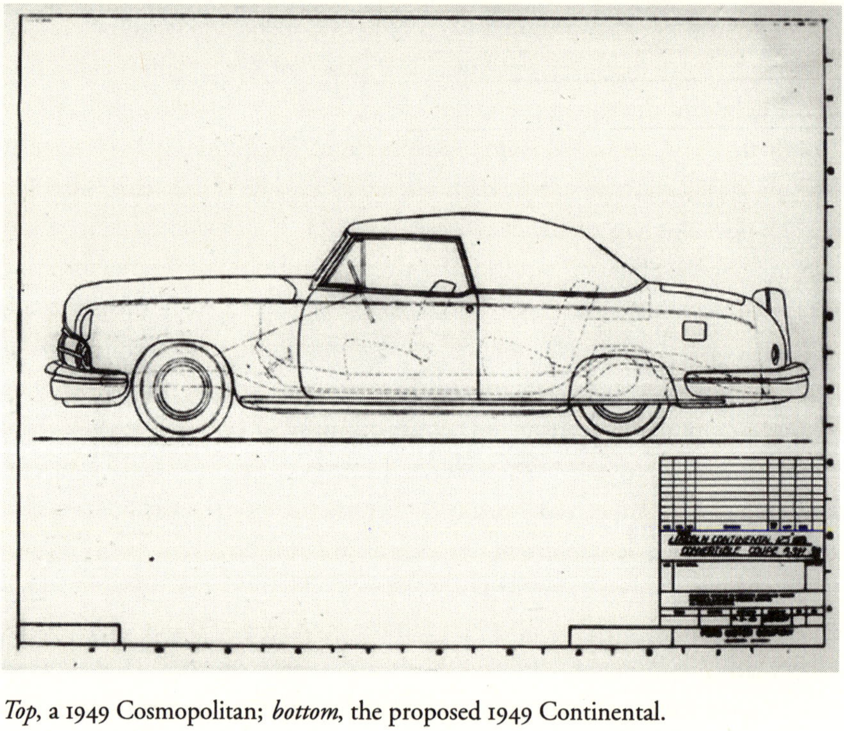

Top, a 1949 Cosmopolitan; *bottom*, the proposed 1949 Continental.

The designs for the Mercury, the small Lincoln and the Lincoln Cosmopolitan were, however, pretty well locked in at this stage. A 1949 Continental was proposed but never really had much of a chance. For one thing, it just didn't look right on the slab-sided 1949 bodies. For another, its chief patron was no longer alive. A series of custom bodies was similarly proposed (designed by Brunn), but dropped.

The Lincolns and Cosmopolitans were revised only slightly in 1950 and 1951. The controversial "frowning" grille of the 1949 design was dealt with for 1950 and the rear end styling was touched up for 1951. These cars stand as monuments to Gregorie's ideas and, to a lesser extent, to those of Edsel Ford. In particular, the fastback Cosmopolitan town sedan of 1949 is a car Edsel Ford would surely have favored had he lived.

The 1949-series Lincolns were among the most important in the marque's history, not simply because they were entirely new cars but because they marked an entirely new marketing direction. They were the first wave of a determined assault on the mainstream of the American luxury car market, a market in which the Lincoln had never had much success or, to any significant extent, ever competed. Lincoln had produced damn-the-cost, custom-built luxury cars in the form of the fabulous L and K models, upper-medium priced cars in the form of the Zephyr and specialty luxury cars in the form of the first series Continentals, but until the 1949 model year had never gone after the mass market luxury buyers.

There were actually two Lincoln cars announced on April 22, 1948, in some ways similar, in some ways quite different. The standard Lincoln was the successor to the Lincolns of the immediate past. It shared the new Mercury body and rode on a 121-inch wheelbase. In price it was about $600 above the Mercury and in a class with the Buick Roadmaster and the Chrysler New Yorker. The newest Lincoln, the Cosmopolitan, was built on a substantially larger body which it shared with no other line and rode on a 125-inch wheelbase. In price it was placed between the popular Cadillac Series 62 and the flagship Fleetwood Series 60 Special.

Both Lincolns had entirely new bodies. They were similar in appearance, especially from the front. The main distinguishing features included the Cosmopolitan's one-piece curved windshield, bold slab sides, and chrome spears over the front wheel cut-outs. The Cosmo was quickly dubbed the "water buffalo," a term used (mostly) with affection. The standard Lincoln had a conventional two-piece windshield and a vestigial front fender line in common with the Mercury. Both models had odd recessed headlights. The original idea had been to employ retractable headlight covers similar to those on the 1942 De Soto, but these were abandoned as the car neared production when engineering determined that they could not be made to function reliably. It was considered to be too expensive at that point to redesign the front end for normal headlight placement, so little tunnels were built to extend back to the recessed lights. Such were the circumstances under which the new Lincolns were designed!

The main feature of the front end, however, was the massive, drooping, and perhaps slightly menacing grille. Ford executives decided they did not like it and it was one of the few major changes authorized for the 1950 model run. Still, the distinctive grille treatment, together with the slab sides and the sheer bulk of the new cars, gave them, and particularly the Cosmopolitan, a vivid, impressive appearance. Whatever else one might say about their styling, it did not permit them to move about unnoticed.

Seven models were offered. The standard Lincoln was available in three body styles: a four-door sport sedan, a two-door six-passenger coupe and a convertible. The Cosmopolitan was available in those three body styles plus a fastback four-door town sedan. This latter body style was a favorite of both E. T. Gregorie and Edsel Ford, but never caught on with the public. General Motors discovered the same thing when it fielded virtually two full lines of fastbacks and notchbacks in 1949: the paying customers vastly preferred notchback styling. The Cosmopolitan town sedan was not continued over for the 1950 model run, and while it is not known precisely how many were built extremely few have survived.

Both Lincolns were powered by the same all-new V8 engine, the first V8 in a Lincoln since 1932. This 336.7 cubic inch engine had been under design since 1941 as an automotive powerplant. Ironically, it got its start in 1948 in the F-7 and F-8 Ford Trucks and played a crucial role in establishing the Ford Truck line as a serious contender in the medium- and heavy-duty commercial markets. It was less successful as a Lincoln engine.

In the first place, there was nothing modern about it; it was simply a nice, big flathead V8 in the Ford tradition and so did not represent any sort of major selling point (other than to the extent that it was not the V12). In the second place, the industry was about to be overwhelmed by a rash of genuinely important new V8 engines. This was particularly true in the fine car field as Cadillac introduced its landmark high compression, overhead-valve V8 in 1949 and Chrysler introduced its magnificent hemispherical combustion chamber V8 in 1951. Against them, the Lincoln V8 was heavy and slow, and uninspiring.

It was the largest engine of its time and it was also very heavy, reportedly exceeding the weight of the 1949 Cadillac V8 by some 200 pounds. Despite its size, it was—as Lincoln owners soon learned—no match for the smaller, lighter Cadillac powerplant. The V8 also suffered from a disproportionate number of design "bugs" when it was first unveiled and thus earned something of a shaded reputation—not so bad as the old V12, but bad enough to be a liability. Still, for all its faults, this engine, like the V12 before it, was splendid for high-speed cruising. Traveling salesmen loved it. It also mated exceptionally well with GM's Hydra-Matic automatic transmission when that became available on the Lincoln in June, 1949. (Ford engineering had not had time to develop its own automatic, and was forced to go outside the company to find one.) In addition, it could boast of aluminum pistons. The exhaust systems running from the cylinder banks were located outside the "V" to allow for more efficient placement of accessories and better access to the engine in general. It was a dramatic improvement in almost every way over the old V12 and, if it was not the fastest thing on the block, at 152 horsepower it was definitely no slouch.

The two Lincolns were much the same underneath. Both used the new Ford "K" type frame and both featured independent front suspensions—at last. The rear axle was of a new semi-floating type, and Hotchkiss drive with hypoid gears made it possible for designers to lower the car considerably. Braking was also improved substantially.

The 1949 Cosmopolitan design studio clay as it appeared in June, 1945.

1949 Cosmopolitan Town Sedan.

Interior trim was similar in the two series. The Cosmopolitan was notable mostly for having certain items standard that were optional on the standard Lincolns, such as hydraulic window lifts, hydraulic seat control and automatic overdrive. The new curved instrument panel was designed for safety and visibility. Sharp projections were avoided and all instruments were located directly in front of the driver with backlighting for nighttime illumination.

The new Lincolns were created in an environment in which everything around them was in a state of flux. The Ford corporate engineering departments and the Lincoln-Mercury Division itself were literally built from the ground up even as the cars were being built from the ground up . . . and all with a tight deadline. It is hardly surprising under the circumstances that the new cars had their share of problems. There were at least 118 running changes made on the Cosmopolitan alone during the 1949 model run. Most of these dealt with problems of the minor-but-annoying variety. A few were more serious in nature. Early engine blocks were notorious for cracking due to inferior metal alloy. Engineers attempted to solve oil consumption troubles by going to four ring pistons in 1949, then three ring pistons in 1950 before finally determining that the engine itself was fundamentally out of balance. This was cured in the latter part of the 1950 model run. The steering was also a cause for many complaints. It was hard and once again the cause was basic design flaws that were never really fixed until the car was completely redesigned in 1952. Furthermore, the general quality of assembly left a lot to be desired in the early 1949s.

Ford officials, for their part, were not particularly happy with certain features of the new Lincolns. The grille, as has been noted, was universally disliked as were the instrument panel, which was considered drab, and the center opening doors on four-door models. This feature was a carry over from the old Zephyr days, but caused so much executive unhappiness that a tooling estimate was authorized to find out how much it would cost to change it in mid-run. Answer: too much, and so that particular alteration was tabled.

Oddly enough, the working press liked the 1949 Lincolns right from the start. *Newsweek* noted approvingly that it was "new from the tires up, but not radical." *Iron Age* praised the styling for being "conservative—but highly pleasing." Tom McCahill, the dean of American road testers, said the Lincoln was the fastest stock American car he had tested since the 1937 Cord, and proclaimed the standard Lincoln the best buy in the medium priced field.[1]

The public, too, seems to have been fairly well impressed. Lincoln production soared to levels that were unheard of. A total of 73,507 cars were built during the 1949 model run, including 38,384 Lincolns and 35,123 Cosmopolitans.

After a generally successful 1949 model run, the 1950 models were not radically changed. The alterations were limited to those necessitated by shortcomings in the original design. The single most obvious change was up front. Gone by executive fiat was the "drooping" or "frowning" grille that made the 1940 models so distinctive, and controversial, in appearance. The new grille was a simple, yet massive, affair featuring two bold horizontal bars, a vertical center bar and four teeth on either side.

Interior trim was mostly redone for 1950. The principal change was the instrument panel. The old panel had been a source of considerable corporate displeasure and so the 1950 models sported a completely new design of a more modern and much flashier appearance. The 1950 interiors featured new colors and fabrics.

The engine was not substantially revised for 1950, other than the ongoing effort to refine it that has been previously noted. The design and placement of the oil dipstick was changed in response to customer complaints and the engine block contained more alloy than before to deal with cracking problems. In an effort to cure oil consumption troubles the pistons went to three rings instead of four. This wasn't the solution, however, and in the middle of the year the balance of the engines was found to be the problem.

The model line-up underwent major revision. The poor-selling Lincoln convertible and Cosmopolitan town sedan were dropped, leaving five models available at new model announcement. A serious challenge, however, was posed by the new two-door hardtop body style that had been first introduced on the

Cadillac Coupe De Ville, Buick Riviera, and Oldsmobile 98 Holiday in the middle of 1949. Similar models from Chrysler and other competitors began appearing with increasing frequency with the advent of the 1950 model year, and the absence of a Lincoln entry became an important liability. Unfortunately, none of the 1949 Ford Motor Company bodies were deemed by engineers to be possessed of sufficient structural strength to permit satisfactory hardtop styling without prohibitively expensive alterations. Ford Division eventually tried anyway with the 1951 Victoria, but the result was not satisfactory. Instead, all Ford Motor Company lines introduced special luxury coupes in the middle of the 1950 model run. The Lincoln entry was the Lido, while the Cosmopolitan model was dubbed the Capri. Both models were offered in a limited selection of colors carefully harmonized inside and out with matching vinyl tops. Upholstery designs featured beautiful cloth and leather combinations.

Production was down in 1950 even taking into account the unusually long 1949 model run. This might have been due to the fact that the cars were no longer quite so dramatically "new" as they had once been. It is also possible that part of the decline was traceable to unfavorable publicity generated by the various flaws inherent in the 1949 design. In any case, a total of 28,190 Lincolns were manufactured in the 1950 model run, including 17,489 Lincolns and 10,741 Cosmopolitans.

The most famous 1950 Lincolns were those in a fleet of custom-built vehicles supplied to the White House. There were no less than ten of them, nine of which were enclosed limousines and one of which was an open parade car. The actual body construction was done by the Henney Motor Company of Freeport, Illinois.

The limousine assigned to the president was built on a special 145-inch wheelbase, and was nearly a ton heavier than the standard Cosmopolitan sedan. It came fitted with special grille lights and running boards for Secret Service agents, although these were later removed because the vehicle had difficulty negotiating the narrow entrances to certain Washington buildings. Mechanically, it was pretty much stock except for its heavy duty Hydra-Matic transmission. The roof line, though, was unusually high to permit the wearing of top hats, still a necessary part of formal attire at the time. The exterior of the car was solid black and the roof was covered with pyroxalyn landau grain-coated fabric. The passenger compartment had its own fresh air heater and radio. Brown lizard skin cases that recessed into the sides of the rear compartment concealed thermos bottles, writing supplies with a gold pen included, plus cigars and cigarettes. The upholstery was gray shadow-stripe broadcloth, as was a matching lap robe. All interior hardware and trim, even down to the door sill plates, were gold-finished. The eight other limousines were similarly fitted, although without the gold-finished trim and minus the special running boards.

The tenth Cosmopolitan, the parade car, was also built on a 145-inch chassis. The coachwork was done under the direction of Raymond H. Dietrich, a famed coachbuilder from the classic era. After the war, he had re-established his own coachbuilding firm in Grand Rapids, Michigan, and one of the first assignments he received was for this car. The master stylist's touch was evident

Top, the 1950 parade car with its 1954 bubbletop in place. *Bottom*, the rear compartment of one of the Henney-built 1950 enclosed limousines.

in the design of the cars. An almost full rear wheel cut-out together with a fender molding similar to the one in front did a remarkably effective job of breaking up the awful visual mass of the vehicle, which could have been truly horrendous given the "bathtub" styling of the Cosmopolitan. A continental tire was mounted at the back atop an enormous wrap-around rear bumper which doubled as the step plates for the Secret Service agents, and also served to increase the visual length. Other than red lights and flag holders at the front, there was not much else non-stock about the exterior appearance. The finished car was twenty feet long and weighed 6,450 pounds.[2]

The 1951 civilian models were further refined editions of the 1949 cars, the most important change being a restyled rear end. This involved some new sheet metal, but was hardly cosmic in its impact. Still, the total effect was noticeable and these models are generally considered to be the finest of the 1949–51 series.

The biggest news on the standard Lincolns was the restyling of the new fin-type rear fenders with vertical tail lights replacing the old round units. The rear window was also considerably enlarged—by as much as 29 percent, according to Lincoln press information.[3] This necessitated a major revision in the roof sheet metal. A new rear box section cross-sill was added to reinforce the body structure and the gas tank filler housing was redesigned, as well.

1950 Cosmopolitan interior.

These changes were shared with the less expensive Mercury line, but the Lincolns managed to retain their own distinctive appearance.

The big Cosmopolitans, too, were restyled, although not to the extent that the smaller series was. The most controversial modification was the addition of a bold—these cars are not remembered for their subtlety—side molding extending the full length of the car and deliberately designed to emphasize the already considerable visual length. It was felt by some that this molding interfered with the cleanliness of the design. The Cosmopolitans had new tail lights similar in style to those on the revised standard Lincolns.

Both Lincolns sported new grilles of a simplified horizontal bar wrap around bumpers. The standard Lincoln also used a new rear bumper made necessary by the new rear fender design. Both cars had new rear deck ornaments and front fender ornaments. The fender ornaments were of an unusual, reverse-fin design.

The engine was increased in horsepower and now stood at 154. An effort was made to eliminate engine vibration and noise by selectively fitting each main crankshaft bearing and valve tappet. Lingering problems with oil consumption were addressed with modified lubrication and an improved valve chamber oil drainage system. Cooling at the exhaust port valves was also improved by use of directional flow tubes.

1950 coupe.

1951 Cosmopolitan.

The model line-up was unchanged over 1950. Prices, however, were up by about 7 percent. The smaller Lincolns were still highly competitive with other makes in the medium priced field and Lincoln salesmen were urged to go after this market. They were instructed to present the standard Lincoln as a "major body change, not just a facelift" even though it was, in fact, just a facelift—and a fairly minor one at that. This emphasis on the standard series was a classic case of the old salesman's adage about selling what you've got. The medium price class Lincolns were due to be dropped for good effective with the beginning of the 1952 model year.

The smaller Lincolns did earn one last bit of glory, however, when they won the 1951 Mobilgas Economy Run with a hard to believe 25.48 mpg. Many people, in fact, refused to believe it but *Motor Trend* magazine managed to virtually duplicate the results with the same car for the July, 1951, issue. The "secret" was a low 3:31 rear axle, plus a high altitude carburetor. The big Cosmopolitan, with the same engine, fared rather poorly in the economy run finishing behind both the Cadillac and the Chrysler Imperial with a 17.123 mpg figure.

Lincoln production, and especially that of the Cosmopolitan, was up over the 1950 total. Cosmopolitan production rose by almost 50 percent to 15,813 while the standard Lincoln was down just a shade at 16,761 for a grand total of 32,574.

The 1949-Series Lincolns and Cosmopolitans were quite popular when they were first announced in April, 1948. The reception soon faded as Cadillac announced its new V8 in 1949 and its second entirely new postwar bodies in 1950. Lincoln was not the only upper bracket marque to suffer under Cadillac's repeated blows, but Ford executives as well as Lincoln-Mercury dealers, were exceedingly unhappy with the way things were turning out and began to look eagerly toward the next new models scheduled for 1952 as being the real push that the 1949s should have been. The 1949s did, however, represent an important new direction of the marque. For the first time ever Lincoln had a range of cars in the bread-and-butter luxury car market opposite the Cadillac Series 62. If they were not sufficiently stunning to take the market by storm, they were at least a foundation upon which to build.

It is also worth noting that 1949–51 Lincolns are gaining adherents among Lincoln enthusiasts as the years go by. They really were much better cars than many Ford and Lincoln-Mercury executives gave them credit for being at the time. Their styling has endured better than that of many of their competitors and the mechanical bugs that marred the early production examples don't seem quite so cosmic in retrospect. Perhaps the real problem was that too much was expected of them.

CHAPTER THREE

Crossing the finish line in the 1953 Mexican Road Race.

Road Racers: 1952–55

THE 1952 LINCOLNS announced on February 6, 1952, were the second completely new cars bearing the name to be produced in four years. As with the 1949 models, the 1952s were not only physically new in practically every important respect, but also represented another stage in Lincoln's development as a serious luxury contender. Moreover, the smaller, medium price Lincolns were not carried over from 1951, thus closing the books on a fifteen-year checkered career in that field. Instead, Lincoln's commitment to the exclusive manufacture of cars of the highest quality was reinforced by the introduction of an entirely new series of luxury cars under the Capri nameplate as upscale companions to the established Cosmopolitans.

It was little wonder, considering the numbers of talented people snatched away from General Motors during the postwar rebuilding of the Ford Motor Company, that all of Ford's first completely postwar designed cars had a marked GM influence. This was especially true in engineering, but was obvious in the styling of the 1952 models, as well, and Lincoln was no exception. The bold, vertical louver gracing the side contour of the new Lincolns had an unmistakable Cadillac quality about it, as did the new tail light treatment. The Lincoln did not go so far as to grow miniature P-38 tail fins—in imitation of Cadillac's imitation—but the new tail light treatment, although minus the fin and considerably increased in size, also had a definite Cadillac quality to it. Doors were all hinged in the front as were those on the Cadillac (and on every other American car for that matter), and Lincoln at long last had a very attractive two-door hardtop. This was a line clearly intended to win converts from the competition, and in the luxury field that meant Cadillac first and foremost.

The general corporate styling themes for 1952 were laid down by George Walker, then operating as a design consultant to Ford. The curvaceous Gre-

A pair of 1952 Capris. *Top*, a convertible; *bottom*, a coupe.

gorie styling gave way to an angular approach that served to unite the entire product line. William Schmidt and Don DeLaRossa were assigned to prepare the specific Lincoln designs.

The styling of the new Lincoln bodies was unusually clean. In fact, it was so clean it was almost plain, and Lincoln stylists would soon be cluttering up their pride and joy in an attempt to make it "look" more expensive. The front end was an evolutionary development of 1950 and 1951 styling. Headlights were once more in a normal position, but recessed rings encircled each headlight as if in homage to the old design. The fenders were quite high, higher even than the hood, and the hood itself had a modern, flat contour.

The most striking feature of the front end, however, was the front bumper design. The bumper wrapped around to the front wheel cut-outs and was made up of two heavy bars, the upper one doubling as the main grille bar. Mercury used a similar concept, although not nearly as attractively done, and they share honors for being the first American cars to pioneer a soon-to-be-ubiquitous new style. It dramatically raised the visual reference points of the front ends of the cars. The parking lights were built into the bumper, and this, too, was a first.

Another interesting innovation around back was a unisex gas tank filler pipe located behind a spring operated license plate bracket. Gasoline could now be pumped from either side of the car for greater convenience. The trunk—with its 30.9 cubic feet of capacity—was 29 percent greater than the old Lincoln and 50 percent greater than the old Cosmopolitan. Despite being more commodious than before, the new bodies looked much lighter. Part of this was due to the increased glass—around 20 percent more than in 1951 on most models—and the thinner windshield pillars. Part of it was due to the fact that the cars were, in fact, lighter—by 300 pounds in the case of the 1952 Cosmopolitan. The new 123 inch wheelbase was an even split of the old 121-inch Lincoln and 125-inch Cosmopolitan wheelbases. In contrast, the 1952 Cadillac 62 rode on a 126-inch wheelbase, and the Chrysler New Yorker used a king-sized 131-1/2-inch wheelbase.

In fact, the smaller size of the new body shell—mandated by Earle MacPherson at corporate engineering—sent the sales and marketing people at Lincoln-Mercury Division into a panic. The hottest car on the market at the time in terms of performance was the Oldsmobile with its "Rocket" V8, and this was the car MacPherson had used as a reference point in engineering the new Lincoln. The trouble was, the Olds was a medium-priced car that was significantly smaller than the Cadillac—or the 1949-51 Lincolns, for that matter.

The only aspect of the physical car over which Lincoln-Mercury had any real authority was the interior, so they set to work with a vengeance to do everything possible to make the the new Lincoln a tour de force in interior design. Most of the basic interior styling themes of the 1951 models were carried over, but they were executed in a newer, fresher, and far more colorful fashion. Exotic fabrics and fabric-and-leather combinations were offered.

Doors were increased in height for easier entrance and exit, and the seats were redesigned with the same goal in mind. A large transmission shift indicator was now built into the steering wheel column on Hydra-Matic equipped cars, which is to say virtually all cars.

The new Lincolns were also fitted with overhead mounted brake pedals, and were the first American cars to feature them as standard equipment. The pedal was suspended from a bracket between the firewall and the instrument panel. The master cylinder was relocated to a position on the firewall to allow for easier maintenance. The suspended pedals offered many advantages over the old set-up. The new system provided greater foot room and eliminated a hole in the floor through which dirt and noise could enter the passenger compartment. It also reduced the chances of the brake mechanism freezing up or being clogged with dirt.

The engineering of the 1952 Lincolns was at least as dramatically new as the styling. Almost as soon as the 1949 L-head powered cars hit the streets, Lincoln

1952 engine.

engineers were working on a lighter, more efficient, high-compression engine of the modern overhead-valve type. The resulting 1952 engine was 18.5 cubic inches smaller in displacement but had a higher compression ratio and six more horsepower than the 1951 version of the old engine. At 317.5 cubic inches, though, the new Lincoln engine was now the smallest in its class. The Cadillac and Chrysler powerplants were not only larger, but developed 30 and 35 more horsepower, respectively. Lincoln engineers were more concerned with economy of operation than in flat-out acceleration. Still, the new engine had the capacity to produce quite a bit more power than the 160 horsepower of the 1952 version, and later models would begin to take greater advantage of the power potential of the design.

The engine was also designed to be over-square: i.e., to have a stroke less than its bore. Pistons in the new engine traveled 20 percent less distance, and the result was less engine wear and increased durability. Lincoln engineers were particularly proud of the valve lift cam contour. They devoted an entire year to the study of the new design with the aid of electronic differential analyzers. Special attention was also given to maintenance problems. The oil pump was mounted externally for ease of service, and the fuel pump was mounted low toward the front of the engine where it could be cooled by air from the fan.

The single most important feature of the new Lincoln was in the chassis. MacPherson was an internationally known expert on suspensions and saw to it that the 1952 Lincoln would have the best system it was possible to design for a big American luxury car. Thus, Lincoln became the first American car to use ball-joint front suspension in place of the old kingpin system. There were two simple ball-and-socket joints on each front wheel. One connected to the top supporting arm, the other to the bottom supporting arm. The new system was far simpler than the old, reduced grease points from sixteen to four, and made servicing and alignment easier. It also made steering easier and more positive, thus resolving another shortcoming of the 1949 design. The chassis was also notable for its more rigid X-type frame and better brakes. The shocks were larger, too, and the rear shocks were relocated to eliminate axle kick-up during acceleration.

They even built a new Lincoln plant at Wayne, Michigan, to replace the old Warren Avenue factory originally built by the Lelands. The Wayne plant would remain in use as a Lincoln facility until the conclusion of the 1957 model run and would then be shifted over to Edsel production. Twenty years later, however, Lincolns would roll from the Wayne line again in the form of the Lincoln Versailles.

There were five models in the 1952 line up, down from seven in the 1951 model year. The standard Lincolns were discontinued completely and the Cosmopolitan series was reduced from four models to two by the elimination of the Capri coupe and the standard convertible. The Capri became three models, a coupe, a four-door sedan and a convertible. The hardtop coupes were especially attractive and won favor with press and public alike. In a rather confusing bit of advertising ledgerdemain all Cosmopolitans were referred to as Custom models and all Capris were referred to as Special Customs.

The first major press coverage appeared in the February, 1952, issue of *Mechanix Illustrated.* Tom McCahill thought the Capri Special Custom coupe he tested was "magnificent" in nearly every respect. In particular, he thought it the most beautiful Lincoln since the Continental. His only major complaint was the lack of power from the smaller engine. As he put it to Lincoln's engineers, "you made the pants too small."[1]

Another, more extensive, road test appeared in the June, 1952, issue of *Motor Trend.* Walt Woron thought the handling to be the obvious outstanding characteristic of the car. He even had good words to say about the 1952 engine, saying that Lincoln had "taken a step in the right direction—more efficiency from a smaller engine." He predicted, however, that Lincoln would soon be forced by the competition to raise the power output.

An owner survey conducted by Floyd Clymer appeared in the October, 1952, issue of *Popular Mechanics.* Fully 86 percent of the owners rated their cars good or excellent overall and only 5 percent rated them poor. Styling was the best-liked feature with handling a close second. The owners seemed satisfied with the power, but did object to the visual similarity of the Lincolns to other, less costly, Ford lines, i.e., Mercurys. Fully 37 percent of the buyers were not previous Lincoln owners, which indicated that Lincoln was having success in capturing new customers.

Some automotive writers have asserted that the 1952 Lincolns were not well received by the public. As proof they cite the total production figures which show a 15 percent decline over 1951. This is entirely true, but ignores the fact that in the 1952 Lincoln line—in order to concentrate exclusively on the luxury market—had dropped the medium price cars which accounted for 51 percent of the 1951 production total. For this reason, the total 1952 production figures can only be fairly matched against the 1951 Cosmopolitan figures and, by that standard, the 1952 models were a huge success. In a market that was down by 18 percent overall, Lincoln luxury car production was up by a remarkable 72.4 percent. Total 1952 model run production was 27,271. Approximately 11,600 of these were Cosmopolitans and 15,600 were Capris. It was by far the most luxury cars Lincoln had ever sold in one model year and was ample evidence that the plan to establish Lincoln as a serious contender in the luxury market was having real success. It was all the more impressive considering that the 1952 model "year" was a short one—only ten months long, February through November—and the industry was plagued by shortages and restrictions of various kinds due to the Korean conflict.

The 1953 Lincolns announced on December 2, 1952, were little changed in appearance and the two models' years are difficult to tell apart, even for experts. But there were important mechanical refinements not readily apparent to the eye. The most important change was under the hood.

Horsepower was increased by 28 percent to 205 in order to answer complaints about the lack of power of the 1952 Lincolns and also to match the sometimes fanciful power outputs being claimed by the competition. Lincoln engineers credited this accomplishment to the superior breathing of the 1953 engine brought about by half a dozen refinements. These included a four-

1953 Ford Fiftieth Anniversary Lincoln Capri show car.

barrel carburetor, larger intake manifold runners, larger intake valve diameters, higher intake valve lift, higher compression ratio and increased idle vacuum. The new carburetor was unique in that in the lower speed ranges only two of the barrels operated. As additional acceleration was needed the other two barrels were automatically brought into operation. A choke interlock was used to prevent complete closing of the secondary barrels while the engine was being warmed up.

Lincoln also offered an array of power-assist optional equipment for the first time. This included power steering, power brakes and power front seat. The electrically-operated, four-way power seat was an industry first. It worked horizontally and vertically, but did not have the tilt feature that became common in future years. Hydra-Matic was standard for the first time.

Interiors were slightly revised in all models. Upholstery fabric offered included tweeds, friezes, nylon, broadcloth and leather. In commemoration of Ford Motor Company's fiftieth anniversary, a gold medallion was mounted on the instrument panel.

Bodies were not altered at all except for a new two-position check mechanism built into the doors. Other alterations involved trim pieces here and there. A one-piece wrap-around rear window did away with the mullions. The Lincoln name was spelled out in block letters on the hood and the crest was dropped in favor of a new hood ornament.

The model range was identical to that offered the previous year. Production however, was up dramatically, as further proof that Lincoln's bid to increase its share of the luxury market was gaining success. A total of 40,672 Lincolns were built during the model run. Of these, 14,122 were Cosmopolitans and 26,630 were Capris. This represented a 49 percent increase overall and an incredible 157 percent increase over Lincoln's luxury car production alone during the 1951 model year.

Yet, Lincoln was not alone in pursuing an aggressive program in the luxury field. Cadillac was out to nail down the leadership it had wrested from Packard in the 1930s, and the boys on Clark Street—with the weight of General Motors behind them—were not to be taken lightly. Packard, beginning with the James Nance administration in 1952, was out to regain its former position. Nothing was readily apparent except for an appealing new line of Packards for 1951, but Nance would pull one rabbit after another out of the hat beginning with the 1953 model year. Chrysler was out to develop its Imperial line as a major force. The long-wheelbase models—seven-passenger sedans and limousines—had been around forever, but an attractive sedan was made available in 1949 and, for 1951, a full range of models was listed.

Despite the inroads Lincoln had made in the luxury market, Benson Ford, L-M's general manager, was still looking for ways to capture the attention of the public with the performance potential of his new Lincoln line. So when Bill Stroppe asked him to arrange factory support for a team of Lincolns to compete in the Mexican Road Race, a three-car team was quickly approved. Preparation of the cars was handled by Stroppe and Clay Smith, both products of the hot rod movement in the 1930s and 1940s. In 1951, without factory sponsorship, Smith had prepared a 1948 Mercury that Troy Ruttman drove to an impressive fourth place finish. Smith and Stroppe weren't strangers to Lincoln-Mercury Division, either. In the 1952 Mobilgas Economy Run, they had driven a Lincoln to a class win.

The third Mexican Road Race—officially, the 1952 Carrera Panamericana held in November, 1952—actually featured 1953 model cars, leading to a certain amount of confusion over the years regarding which cars were run in which race. The route itself encompassed 1,912 difficult miles, running from Tuxtla Gutierrez in the south to Juarez along the American border.

In contrast to earlier years, the 1952 race was conducted under rules that prohibited the use of non-stock modifications. In theory, an ordinary customer could purchase from his friendly neighborhood Lincoln-Mercury dealer all the equipment required to create a replica of the winning 1953 Lincoln. In fact, the new rules mainly served to keep the cheating down to a dull roar.

Stroppe and Smith borrowed the cam and mechanical valve lifters from the

1953 Capri.

F-8 Ford truck engine (essentially the same engine used in the 1949–51 Lincolns).[2] The intake manifold was reworked for optimum gas flow. The stock four-blade fan was replaced by a three-blade unit. Lincoln-Mercury helped out by listing dual exhausts as optional equipment just prior to the race, but they were never actually used due to the proximity of the left-hand pipe to the fuel pump and the resultant danger of vapor lock. In addition, during pre-race tests it was discovered that the engine cross-over pipe had a tendency to snap at high speeds. A slip joint solved the problem.

Since Lincoln had dropped both its manual three-speed and overdrive transmissions for 1953, the Lincoln race cars were equipped with General Motors-built Hydra-Matic transmissions, as were all "slush-box" Lincolns from 1949–53. The Hydra-Matic units were not modified in any way other than to be adjusted for tolerances and optimum shift points.

Heavy duty "export" springs were used, with dual Houdaille shocks and air lifts added in front. Two heavy-duty Gabriel shocks were fitted at the rear. One hundred Firestone racing tires were sent to Mexico for the race. They were inflated to 45 psi with nitrogen (which was not affected by heat and remained at a constant pressure), and at the end of each day's racing all tires were changed.

Such non-essentials as radio, power steering, power brakes, etc., were jettisoned to save weight. Still, the need to carry forty-one gallons of fuel (some of it in an auxiliary tank located in the rear seat) pushed overall weight past the 4000 pound mark, or about 400 pounds over stock trim. This, in turn, put a heavy burden on the brakes, so a Cop-Sil-Loy coating was applied to the linings and two heater fans mounted in the trunk blew air through ducts onto the rear brakes. These fans operated continually and also helped clear the cockpit of hot air and fumes.

That Smith and Stroppe did their work well is confirmed by the results: The 1953 Lincolns swept the first four places in the production car division. (The fourth car was a non-factory entry driven by Ray Crawford.) Lincoln publicists then went to work seeing to it that the story reached as wide an audience as possible.

In addition to print advertising, every major car magazine in America was given the opportunity to test the 1953 Lincoln. John Bond reported in *Road & Track* (March, 1953): "Great things were expected from this car and we were not disappointed . . . Unquestionably the 1953 Lincoln is the fastest stock car in America." *Motor Trend* (March, 1953) was impressed by the power: "Acceleration does not appear to taper off, as with many cars; it just keeps coming." Dean Batchelor, writing in *Hop Up* (March, 1953) endorsed both the new

Lincolns and Mercurys as being "the best designed mass-produced automobiles in the world."

Hop Up magazine was given the opportunity to test Ray Crawford's actual Mexican Road Race car. The results (again as published in their March, 1953, issue) showed a 116.9 mph top speed and a zero to 60 mph time of 15.4 seconds. This seemed suspiciously slow, possibly due to the rainy weather conditions at the time of the test, and *Hop Up* was at pains to include the views of Bill Stroppe who reported: "We found that the Lincoln would run about 120 to 125 mph depending on the smoothness of the road, wind and how level the road was."

Still, it seems likely that the Lincoln was the best all-around American performance car in 1953. This was due to a combination of high top speed, good acceleration (especially in the upper speed ranges), relatively modest weight, and superior handling. These qualities, plus the talent of Clay Smith, made Lincoln virtually invincible. It was a public relations grand slam and Lincoln sales soared. Benson Ford had gotten his money's worth.

Yet, the competition was not standing still, either. While they may not have had Latin American races to boast about, all of Lincolns competitors were actively expanding their product ranges in 1953. Cadillac introduced the first of what was to become the long-running Eldorado series that year. Packard countered with a semi-custom convertible called the Caribbean, and Chrysler finally equipped its Imperial line with an automatic transmission.

Lincoln did build a special convertible in 1953, but it was strictly intended for the car show circuit. Designed to commemorate Ford Motor Company's Fiftieth Anniversary, it was finished in striking gold-and-white. Exterior paint was gold metallic, while the interior was entirely in white—including leather upholstery, carpets and painted surfaces. All the hard trim inside and out was done up in gold finish. It wasn't subtle and wasn't meant to be. This model might have made an interesting alternative to the Cadillac Eldorado and Packard Caribbean, but it was never considered for series production.

The 1954 Lincolns were announced on December 3, 1953, just in time for a nationwide recession. Perhaps of more importance, arch rival Cadillac was ready with an entirely new body. All that Lincoln dealers had to fight this double dose of bad news was a slightly facelifted version of a car that would be three years old. It was a measure of their ability and the inherent quality of their product (and the public's perception thereof) that they were able to come very close to matching 1953's record production. Sales of the more expensive Capri line actually increased.

There were no especially important mechanical changes for 1954. Exterior styling was modified in a mild sort of way. No sheet metal was changed, but there was some new trim in various places—mostly in the front end. An interesting feature of the new frontal design was the pair of aggressively styled bumper guards. These were known in the trade as "dagmars" because of a marked resemblance to the physical attributes of a television starlet of the period. A smaller set of dagmars graced the rear bumper. Lincoln would say only that the new bumper guards gave the 1954 Lincoln a "forward thrust."[3] Indeed.

Interior changes were mostly limited to the use of new colors and patterns. The number of models that were offered was unchanged from 1953.

Production in the 1954 model run declined slightly to 36,993. Of this number 7,441 were Cosmopolitans and 29,522 were Capris. Considering the competition provided by the new Cadillac line, the 1954 Lincoln totals were truly impressive.

More good news came from the 1953 Mexican Road Race, which started on November 19, 1953. It followed the same route as in 1952, and was run under a new set of even more stringent regulations intended to further distinguish between out-and-out racing machines and true stock cars. As a result, some of the tricks Lincoln had employed in 1952—the truck cam and solid lifters, for example—were outlawed. Equally important was a requirement that all cars be impounded each night within three hours after the finish of the day's racing to prevent major repairs from being made. The race was becoming a true test of the stamina of fundamentally stock automobiles.

1954 Capri.

If these changes seriously hampered Clay Smith and his fleet of Lincolns, it didn't show. Lincoln scored another grand slam, filling not only the top four slots but—owing to a number of successful private entries—the eighth, ninth and tenth places, as well. Chuck Stevenson and Clay Smith won with the very same Lincoln that had been victorious in 1952. "In the history of American automobile racing," wrote Griff Borgeson in *Hop Up* magazine (February, 1954), "the perfection of the Lincoln organization before and during the fourth Panam has never been equalled."

The appearance of Lincoln in the 1954 Mexican Road Race was a foregone conclusion. It was not quite like old times, though; a freak accident early in September at a race at DuQuoin, Illinois, had taken the life of Clay Smith. There was considerable doubt that the Lincolns would be able to repeat their 1952 and 1953 spectaculars without his guiding hand. And, indeed, on the very first leg of the race—the grueling 329 mile stretch between Tuxtla Gutierrez and Oaxaca—five Lincolns fell by the wayside. Fourteen Lincolns had been entered in the sedan class (including non-factory cars), but after just one day four of the factory cars had been eliminated, leaving only those of Bill Faulkner and Bill Vukovich in the running.

On the second day, Vukovich crashed and the mighty Lincoln team was down to one car—Faulkner's—plus a private entry driven by Ray Crawford that had been given access to the team's facilities. Crawford was a veteran of the Mexican events, but had never finished better than eighth. This time, his

1954 Capri interior.

1954 Capri.

surprising victory not only climaxed his racing career, but saved the day for Lincoln. Lincoln's arch enemies over on Clark Street had very nearly grabbed the prize; Keith Andrew, driving a 1954 Cadillac, won the two fastest legs of the race and finished just three minutes behind Crawford.

Unfortunately, the 1954 event was the end of the line for the Mexican Road Race. The deaths of several drivers and spectators had aroused a reaction against it. Meanwhile, Olds and Hudson had discovered stock car racing north of the border—Olds with its wonderful Rocket V8, Hudson with an archaic flathead six that was fabulously tweaked with multiple carbs and anything else a failing company could throw into the brew. It wasn't good enough to save Hudson, but Lincoln, Olds and Hudson between them had made stock car racing respectable and opened the gates to big-buck sponsorship. The sport never looked back and neither did Detroit.

For Lincoln, its racing activities had helped propel the make to its highest level of public recognition and market penetration ever. One wonders how much the whole effort cost Benson Ford. Figures haven't survived, but, considering the costs of racing in those simpler days, it must have been peanuts compared to the enormous public relations benefits that Lincoln accrued. In fact, the Mexican Road Race experience was one of the great public relations triumphs in the postwar history of the industry and a classic example of a brilliant promotional effort.

Lincoln did not have a particularly good year in 1955, either. Although the industry as a whole was producing more cars than ever before in its history, Lincoln was hampered by an aging design and the stiffest competition it had yet faced in its postwar resurgence as a serious luxury contender. Cadillac had introduced a new and highly successful car in 1954. Packard and Imperial (now a separate marque) had bold new cars ready for the 1955 model year. All were bigger, flashier and more powerful than the 1955 Lincoln.

Lincoln's bold, new car would not be ready until the 1956 model run, and so the car Lincoln dealers had for sale on new model announcement day, November 23, 1954, was a warmed-over stop-gap. Still, it represented the most important change yet in the 1952 design and included a number of interesting features.

By far the most important development was the announcement of Lincoln's exclusive automatic transmission. Known as Turbo-Drive, the new transmission supplanted the GM Hydra-Matic transmission that had been in use on Lincoln cars since the middle of the 1949 model year. Turbo-Drive was a combination of a hydraulic torque converter and planetary gearing. Although Turbo-Drive was a three-speed transmission, it operated as a two-speed under normal driving conditions. Normally, it started in the intermediate gear and shifted automatically into high. Low range could be engaged by means of a throttle kickdown during maximum acceleration. Under hard acceleration the transmission would shift automatically into intermediate gear at about 35 miles an hour and into high gear at about 75 miles an hour. Low gear could also be manually selected. The shift pattern, left to right, was park, reverse, neutral,

1955 Cosmopolitan.

drive and low—or "PRNDL" (pronounced "prindle") and later became the industry standard. Thus, it was not necessary to pass through a forward gear to reach reverse, as on Hydra-Matic.

The 1955 version of the Lincoln overhead-valve V8 included numerous improvements over the 1952-54 engine. Bore was increased to 3.94, resulting in an increase in cubic displacement to 341. The compression ratio was increased from 8.0 to 8.5. As a consequence, horsepower was upped from 205 to 255. This was not enough to match power quotes from other luxury car makers, but it made a difference in the way the Lincoln performed. Also of note, dual exhausts were standard equipment for the first time, and tire tubes disappeared for good with the advent of modern tubeless tires.

A couple of important accessories were first introduced in 1955. One of these was air conditioning. This early Lincoln unit was trunk mounted. The air intakes were affixed to the rear quarter panels and regulated by levers on the rear package tray. The cool air outlets were located along the tops of the side windows with two on either side.

Another intriguing accessory, known as Multi-Luber, was an automatic lubrication system operated from a push button mounted on the instrument panel. It consisted of a master cylinder located in the engine compartment from which nylon tubing extended to each front end chassis bearing. On the tip of each tube was a coupling which fit over the regular grease fitting, and at the press of the dash button lubricating grease was forced through the tubes to provide lubrication of the chassis, suspension and steering systems.

The Lincoln body bore the largest number of alterations since it was introduced in 1952, including the first sheet metal changes. In styling terms, the 1955 Lincoln was a bridge between the 1952–1954 design and the upcoming 1956 one. The thin horizontal bars in the grille and the dramatically canted fins on the rear end previewed major 1956 themes. The rear quarter panels were eight inches longer, giving the car an odd, tail-heavy look, although the actual length of the car was increased by less than an inch. As if this weren't sufficient, the gravel guards were redesigned to make the rear end appear even longer. New projecting headlight bezels were featured on the front end (more visual length!) and the interior was revised with new colors and patterns.

The model line-up was the same as that offered in 1954. The Cosmopolitan name, however, was dropped. The base series was now simply the Lincoln. The Lincoln Capri series remained unchanged. Although the industry as a whole enjoyed record production in 1955, Lincoln was down by almost 27 percent to 27,222 cars. Of these 23,673 were Capris and a mere 3,549 were base models.

The early postwar era was a time of tremendous upheaval and competitiveness in the luxury market, rivaled only by the early years of the depression. This is what Lincoln was up against as it sought to establish itself, almost from scratch, as a full-line luxury car producer. It was not a modest goal, but Lincoln designers and engineers had proved in 1952 that if you produced the goods for your dealers, your dealers could do the rest. Lincoln's luxury class production nearly quadrupled between 1950 and 1953. Its penetration of the fine car field rose to better than 22 percent. In 1956, they hoped to do even better.

CHAPTER FOUR

1956 Premiere convertible interior.

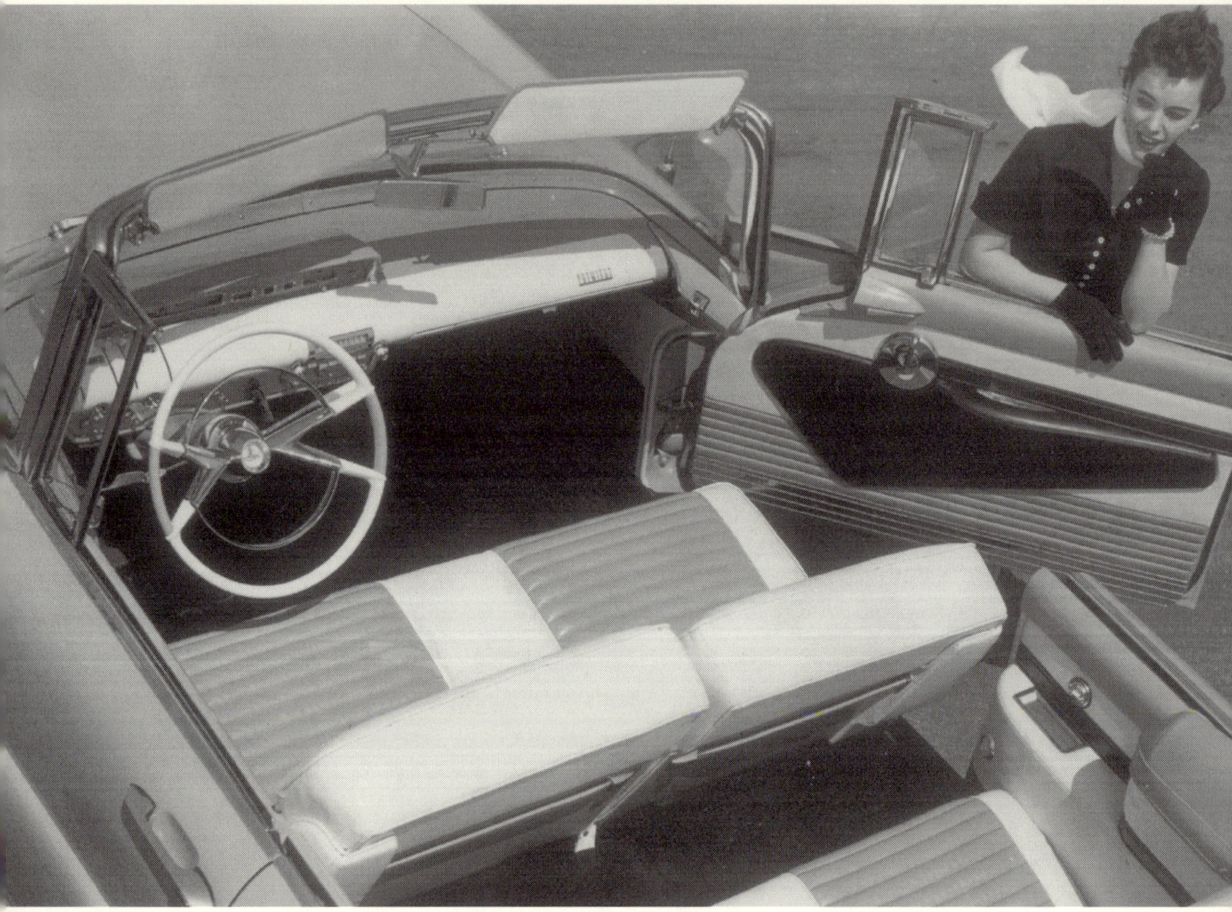

A Tale of Two Lincolns: 1956–57

THERE WERE REALLY TWO Lincoln stories for 1956—Lincoln and Continental—and their respective fates spoke volumes about the ruinous level of internal politics in Ford Motor Company in the 1950s. Almost immediately upon assuming the helm in 1945, Henry Ford II decided that the only way to resurrect Ford Motor Company was to emulate the General Motors model. Significantly, one of his first major decisions was to hire Ernest R. Breech, then being groomed to head GM. Breech, in turn, hired away many General Motors executives for a variety of top positions at Ford, including Earle S. MacPherson. MacPherson was an empire-building engineer who turned the corporate engineering staff at Ford into his personal fiefdom.

Henry Ford II also hired a group of ten former Army Air Force officers who had acted as advisors to the military during the war in statistical analysis, cost-benefit analysis, cost controls, and so on—skills Ford Motor Company desperately needed. He hired them in toto and immediately turned them loose on an unsuspecting company, where they proceeded to develop the financial staff into another power center in opposition to MacPherson and Breech. They came to be known as the Whiz Kids and were led by Robert S. McNamara.

Meanwhile, Lincoln-Mercury executives had discovered the secrets of the

1950 General Motors interchangeability program—although it took them until 1952 to do so. Richard Stout, a recent arrival from GM, spilled the beans. This led to a detailed proposal to Ford Motor Company management for a dramatic expansion of the Mercury product range by means of sophisticated body interchangeability—a proposal that set in motion events that would ultimately result in— among other things—the Edsel.[1] That, in turn, enraged McNamara and his Whiz Kids (on the one hand) and McPherson (on the other) who couldn't agree about much of anything, but were furious that the sales and marketing types at Lincoln-Mercury would have the temerity to mess around in product planning. Old Lincoln-Mercury hands insisted for years that McPherson wreaked his vengeance by delaying the next important Lincoln product launch—i.e., that the celebrated 1956 line had originally been scheduled for 1955.

McPherson's determination to control product planning with an iron grip has been cited as a key reason the other big Lincoln story that year involved a separate division entirely, and, moreover, one with its own engineering department. So the second generation Continental Mark II was not officially a Lincoln at all, although everyone regarded it as such. How could a car bearing the legendary name not be?

The Continental Mark II was the outgrowth of Special Product Operations organized in July, 1952, under the leadership of William Clay Ford. The name was changed to the Special Product Division in October, 1953. The Continental was transferred over to the newly created Continental Division on April 19, 1955, still under the direction of William Clay. At the same time, Ben D. Mills assumed the front office in the newly divorced Lincoln Division, and, just to confuse the lines of authority a bit more, William Clay was named group director for both Lincoln and Continental Divisions. (Presumably, part of his functions as group director was to monitor his own performance as head of the Continental Division!) The Continental Division, in any case, was discontinued after July 21, 1956. It was then merged with Lincoln under Mills' management. William Clay went on to direct corporate product planning and styling.

Because of all the attention focused on the Continental—both then and now—the standard Lincoln line was somewhat overshadowed and, to a certain extent, an unsung tour de force. This is a shame, because the 1956 Lincoln was everything the road race Lincolns had been in the engineering department—even better in the opinion of many observers—and endowed with styling that was little shy of stunning. The 1956 Lincoln was quite possibly the best looking American car in volume production that year, and one of the finest of the decade.

The standard Lincoln was derived in large part from a couple of Lincoln-Mercury show cars, the XL-500 and the Futura. Both were designed by Lincoln stylist William Schmidt. Schmidt also did the exteriors for the 1956 Lincolns. Interiors were mostly done under the supervision of Hermann Brunn, and they, too, were gorgeous. Mechanically, the 1956 Lincoln chassis was heavily revised from the 1955 version, the engine in particular receiving a major reworking.

It was, in all, the most competitive package Lincoln had ever fielded, and its position was enhanced still further by the fact that it was the only really new offering in the luxury market in 1956. Sales and production soared to an all-time record pace and total industry penetration reached a level that would not be matched until the early 1970s.

The 1956 Lincolns were announced to the public on September 8, 1955, with the Continental Mark IIs following in October. The Lincolns were available in two series, the Capri and the new Premiere. Now, for the first time, Lincoln had Cadillac's most popular models covered one for one. Capri models were priced with the Cadillac Series Sixty-Two models, while Premieres were priced with the new Cadillac Series Sixty-Two De Villes. While Ford engineering had not had time to prepare a four-door hardtop model to counter that of the De Ville, the Lincoln and Cadillac body types were otherwise closely matched. Moreover, the Lincolns were almost entirely new while the Cadillacs were forced to make do with a third-year facelift. After the dealer preview showing of the new cars, Lincoln Division was flooded with a record number of orders.

The 1956 Lincoln body and chassis were completely new, and much larger. The Lincolns had for years been the smallest cars in their field, but that was a problem Lincoln-Mercury dealers no longer needed to confront. The new models were seven inches longer, two inches wider and rode on a three inch longer wheelbase than in 1955. At 222.8 inches in length, the new Lincoln was one of the longest cars in the industry, while, at 60.2 inches in height, it was one of the lowest.

In contrast to the slightly odd 1955s, the 1956 Lincolns were beautifully proportioned. Most of the old themes were carried over, but this time they worked famously. These cars are text book examples of the stylists' power to create images. The mental impressions one retains of the 1955 and 1956 models are totally different, yet if the actual cars are examined in detail it is obvious that, feature for feature, they are startlingly similar. There were, however, a number of detail changes.

While the front end design was basically the same, the 1956 did away with the old dagmar bumper guards and replaced them with flattened, rectangular guards that contained the built-in parking lights. The new headlight hoods were equally unusual, having been lifted bodily from the Lincoln Futura show car. The 1955 side molding was gone, and the 1956 sides were left beautifully unadorned except for a horizontal crease in the sheet metal. The awkward gravel shields on the 1955s were discarded and replaced by a simple spear type molding extending from the rear bumper to the front wheels. It served to accentuate visual length of the car without being ostentatious.

The rear fender fins and tail lights were almost identical in design to those on the 1955 model, but the rear bumper design was new. Dual exhaust outlets were built into the new "jet-pod" rear bumper guards, the back-up lights were concealed beneath the lip of the rear deck lid, and the area between the deck lid and the bumper had its own "grille" composed of thin, horizontal bars. This tied the two ends of the car together thematically and also served to heighten its visual width.

Most trim ornaments were similar in design to those used in 1955. One odd feature of the 1956 design was a little triangular rear quarter window on four-door models. The new "sweep around" windshield was billed as having more glass area than any other fine car.

Most of the upholstery patterns and trim pieces were of a new design, but the instrument panel was quite similar to that offered in 1955. The 1956 panel had a lighter "feel" than the old one, but not so light as that on the Mark II (which was, again, a similar design). Power windows and power seats were standard on the new Premieres and power steering was now standard on all Lincolns. Lincoln's optional power brakes were of a new fixed-anchor design. This involved positioning the accelerator and brake pedals in such a way that the driver could pivot his foot easily from one to the other.

Ford was launching a major campaign in 1956 to sell safety to American car buyers. Lincolns did not have padded instrument panels, as did other Ford lines. Still, all but a few early production Lincolns had an unpadded vinyl cover on the instrument panel that at least served to cut down on glare and unwanted reflections. Lincoln did make use of the deep-dish steering wheel idea. Called "safety-flex," it involved recessing the steering wheel hub as a way of preventing driver chest injuries in accidents. Also as a part of the safety package were new double-grip rotor door locks designed to withstand three times normal impact in collisions, and vinyl coating on the rear view mirror to reduce the danger of shattering. Seat belts were also offered, but only about 10 percent of the customers bought them.

A completely new ventilation system was introduced. It increased by 50 percent the amount of air taken into the car for ventilation, heating and defrosting. The dual-control heater used two heating units, one under the instrument panel, the other under the front seat which could be operated separately. Also, the optional air conditioning system—still trunk mounted—was revised to deliver 13 percent more cooled air to the passenger compartment.

Lincoln had a new radio, too, in the list of options. This "travel-tuner" radio included an automatic signal seeking function that could be set on either of two levels of sensitivity. A rear seat radio speaker and an electric antenna were also offered.

The 1956 Lincoln engine was a heavily reworked version of the overhead-valve design introduced on the 1952 models. While it could not accurately be

1956 Capri.

described as a new engine, there was hardly a part in it that escaped some sort of modification. The block, crankshaft, camshaft, oil pump and ventilating system were all new.

The displacement was increased to 368 cubic inches (up 27) and the horsepower rating rose by 27 percent to 285, an increase of 60 horsepower over 1955. The compression ratio was also raised to 9.0 and the torque rating was the highest in the industry. Lincoln engineers calculated that straight line acceleration was improved by 14 percent over the 1955 figures. This was also the year the electrical system was upped from 6 volts to 12 to supply the greater power required by the lengthening list of power accessories.

A new four-barrel carburetor was an improved version of the first fully automatic four-barrel carburetor pioneered by Lincoln on the 1953 models. The two reserve barrels were activated only by the demands of the engine, not by the accelerator, an important fuel economy factor at lower speeds. An unusual feature was a dual intake for carburetor air as part of a temperature controlled air induction system. Rather than take in air from above the engine—air which in summer weather is frequently so hot it is not dense enough to give full power—a fresh air intake was positioned on the left side of the grille to admit cooler outside air. This intake was attached to the air cleaner and operated by a thermostatically controlled flap valve.

The Lincoln Turbo-Drive automatic transmission was continued over from 1955. A modified kickdown feature permitted demand down-shifting into low at all speeds below 70 miles an hour.

The 1956 Lincolns were in their own way even more enthusiastically received by the press and public alike than the dramatic new Continental Mark II. Although the Mark II grabbed most of the attention, the significance of the regular Lincolns was not lost on the automotive writers of the time. Walt Woron and Don MacDonald, writing in *Motor Trend*, noted that these cars represented the "first serious attempt to dislodge Cadillac from its corner on the fine-car market . . . They took a bead on what buyers of luxury automobiles seem to want today, and created same."[2] Woron and MacDonald were almost unanimous in their praise, their only serious reservation being that the handling was not quite up to the old Lincoln standards under hard driving. This they attributed to softer springing.

Tom McCahill, writing in Mechanix Illustrated, disagreed. He felt that the new Lincoln was as good or better than the old one in virtually every respect, even handling. "For 1956, Lincoln has done the impossible: they've built safety and roadability into a huge car. Here is a heavyweight with all the agility and flashy reflexes of the fastest featherweight."[3]

In the middle of the model year, Floyd Clymer published a survey of Lincoln owners in Popular Mechanics. An amazing 84.6 percent of those responding rated their 1956 Lincolns as excellent, and only a minute 2.6 percent rated their cars as poor. This was a significant improvement over the approval rating given the last all new Lincolns in 1952, though that figure was a good one. Almost a third of the owners were first time Lincoln buyers, too, which indicated some success in snaring owners of competitive makes. The things the owners liked best about their cars were the handling, the styling, the performance and the comfort. The things they liked least were the quality of assembly, the number of body rattles and the dealer service. Nearly one-third of the sample reported no complaints of any kind.

In June, the Industrial Designers' Institute in Chicago honored the 1956 Lincoln Premiere hardtop coupe with its outstanding product design award, the first such award to go to automotive designers. Ben D. Mills, general manager of the Lincoln Division, accepted the award.

Lincoln sales made a huge leap in 1956 and production for the model year was up over 84 percent from the 1955 totals. A final figure of 50,322 was reached, a record by a wide margin. Of these, 41,531 were models of the new Premiere series, and 8,791 were Capris. It was a production achievement that would not be equaled for ten years.

And now, as Paul Harvey would say, page two . . .

After the passing of the first Continental in 1948, there was a large residue of feeling both inside and outside the company that a place should be found in future product plans for a Continental-type vehicle. Henry, Benson and William Clay Ford believed that development of such a car would be a fitting tribute to their father, the late Edsel Ford. The idea gained added urgency as the early 1950s battle for supremacy in the luxury car field heated up. Cadillac, as might have been expected, exploded the first bombshell with its Eldorado convertible in 1953. This model was quickly followed by similar models from several other marques: the Packard Caribbean, the Buick Skylark and the Olds Fiesta.

Although it was not appreciated at the time, these cars represented the beginnings of the personal car market in the United States. What was appreciated was that they represented an escalation in the battle for prestige. The Eldorado was not expected by Cadillac executives to add significantly to the total number of Cadillac sales in and of itself. What it was expected to do was add additional luster to the Cadillac name, serve as a further draw for showroom traffic, and thus spur sales of less expensive models. The price Cadillac was charging—and getting—for the Eldorado was something of a shocker.

The Eldo was two thousand dollars higher in price than the Series Seventy-Five limousine and almost twice the price of the Lincoln Capri convertible. Cadillac seemed to be threatening not only a prestige war, but a sort of reverse price war, as well.

The Special Products team under William Clay Ford was prepared to do battle on Cadillac's terms. What they set out to build was a car in the combined traditions of the original Continental (elegant beauty) and the classic K Lincolns (extreme quality and price). John Reinhart was assigned to do the styling. Gordon Buehrig—designer of the legendary Cord 810—was named body engineer, and Harley Copp was named chief engineer. The styling was done independently of regular Lincoln styling. Engineering, on the other hand, was carefully coördinated with Lincoln engineering since the new Continental was not slated to have its own engine or drive-train.

The first Reinhart proposal for the new Continental was ready in the latter months of 1952. It met with decisive rejection from top Ford management, reportedly from Henry Ford II, himself. At that juncture, a styling competition was organized with entries to be submitted by Special Products, George Walker, Vince Gardner, Walter Buell Ford (not connected with the company) and the team of A. B. Grisinger and Reese Miller. Ten designs were submitted, including three related proposals from Special Products. In April, 1953, five members of the Ford Executive Committee independently viewed the proposals and all five voted in a secret ballot for one or the other of the Special Products entries. It was a sweet moment of victory for the "house" team, and this sense of accomplishment was heightened when, on May 12th, William Clay Ford was made a vice-president of Ford Motor Company.

Design work proceeded very quickly from this point. The final car did not, in fact, differ from the Special Products proposals in any great way. Construction on a Continental plant was begun in May, 1954. The first engineering prototype was ready by December, and the first production model was completed on June 24, 1955. Official announcement was made to the public on October 21st.

The original plan called for a growing number of Continental models to follow the coupe, leading up to a full range of super-quality, super-prestige cars that would blow Cadillac out of the water for good. Two such models reached advanced design stages. The first was a retractable hardtop/convertible. The engineering problems inherent in such a concept were numbing, but eventually overcome only to run up against the objection that the modest Continental production volume couldn't justify the investment. The technology was not wasted, though. It reappeared as the basis for the 1957–59 Ford Skyliner retractable. Still, later, it was the basis for the soft-top mechanism used on the 1961–67 Lincoln Continental four-door convertible. The second Continental projected for subsequent production was a four-door hardtop. This car was ultimately restyled to fit into the 1958 Continental Mark III line-up—which was not quite in the same mold as the Mark II, but more on that later.

The Continental Mark II was hailed as an instant classic by practically every news report or road test upon its introduction in the fall of 1955. Everyone seemed to sense that this was a distinctly different sort of car. It was not a flashy, chrome-laden luxury barge. It was not a sports car even in the rather peculiar 1950s meaning of the term (the massive Cadillac Eldorado was promoted as a "sports car"). It was not a rolling laboratory of technical innovations. Ford Motor Company certainly could have made the Continental into anything it wanted to be. What it chose to manufacture was a somewhat sporty personal luxury car of the very highest quality and styled in consummate good taste. And at an astronomical price of nearly $10,000. This was 50 percent more than the most expensive Cadillac in 1956 and $2,000 more than the Ghia-built Imperial Crown limousine.

Like the original Continental, the Mark II was a semi-custom job—if only because of the numbers of vehicles involved—using for the most part standard Lincoln mechanical components. The engine and drive-train were taken right off the regular Lincoln assembly line. While they were checked far more critically for quality control, and in some cases refinished to present a more impressive cosmetic appearance, they were not in any meaningful way special to the Mark II. The strength of the Mark II lay in its unique coachwork and in the sheer quality of its manufacture and assembly.

Basically, the car was designed and styled as a natural successor to the legendary first Continental—the Mark I, if you will, although a numerical designation was never used with it—manufactured from 1939 to 1948. The proportions of the hood, greenhouse and rear deck closely followed that of the first Mark. The Mark II even had an upright spare tire in keeping with the original design, although on the Mark II the tire was concealed beneath a bulge in the rear deck lid instead of being left in the open. The lowness of the Mark II and its proportions necessitated an exclusive "Y" frame with the dual exhausts routed outside the side frame rails as well as a special three-point drive shaft. The Mark II did have one intriguing mechanical innovation: fully automatic, speed-compensating shock absorbers on the front wheels. These operated by means of thermostatically controlled springs to react to the changes in physical action brought about by different driving conditions.

An interesting feature of the Mark II body was its thin pillar windshield construction. The windshield also wrapped around to an unusual degree and was eight inches closer to the driver than normal. This was done to provide increased vision and also to further lengthen the hood. It was also felt that the position would increase the driver's sense that he "belonged" to the car and augment the intimacy of the passenger compartment. The steering wheel was placed in an almost vertical position and the instruments were grouped behind it in a series of four simple, round dials. Gauges included a tachometer and a warning arrow for the fuel gauge. The arrow pointed to the gauge, and as the amount of fuel fell below three gallons, would glow red. The instruments were topped by a leather covered hood design to prevent reflections. In most interior dimensions the Mark II was an inch or two smaller than the Lincoln hardtop. Despite its low silhouette, however, it actually had more headroom and more rear seat hip room.

A wide selection of interior colors and fabrics were available at no extra cost and almost anything could be had on special order, although few such special orders seem to have been made. There were 43 standard upholstery trim

1956 Continental Mark II.

schemes and 19 exterior paint schemes. Interior fabrics included leather, nylon, matelassé, brocade and broadcloth.

It was determined during the development of the Mark II that its hallmark would be the highest level of quality possible in order to obtain in a limited production automobile. In order to attain this goal a seven-point quality control program was devised.

1. Quality Specifications. A decision was made in the early planning stages of the car that the materials and assemblies used should be of the highest practical standards of finish and performance. In many instances it was decided that the best current standards were not good enough and suppliers had to be found who were capable and willing to reach for "newer and higher" standards. Exterior chrome, for example, was expected to pass a 240-hour salt spray test. This was double the industry norm and the only way it was achieved was by special hand metal finishing and an exacting plating process never before used on a production car. Production of certain soft trim parts was held up for months because the manufacturers could not meet the specified standards re-

1956 Continental Mark II.

garding resistance to color bleeding and fading. Leather from Scotland was used because of its extremely high quality, but it was dyed in the United States because American color finishes for leather were better. Exterior paints were chosen for durability even though that meant avoiding some of the flashier (and popular) high metallic content paints that looked great when new but just did not wear well. The Mark II was the only Ford product to use lacquer.

2. Initial Sample Inspection. It was customary in this era for automakers to inspect samples of supplier parts prior to initial shipment in order to ascertain that the parts would fully comply with the manufacturers' specifications. Often, though, in the rush to get a new model into production, this process was compromised or abandoned altogether. In order to avoid this from happening with the Mark II, the initial sample inspections were scheduled six weeks earlier than usual and the initial production itself was scheduled at a deliberately slow pace as an additional safeguard. As it turned out, some initial samples had to be rejected three or four times before they passed inspection and over 50 percent of the initial samples were rejected at least once. Even some experienced automotive suppliers had difficulty maintaining the new standards. This phase of the quality program eventually caused initial production to be delayed, but when the first cars came off the line every one of them was built 100 percent with parts that had been approved.

1956 Continental Mark II interior.

3. Receiving Inspection. All manufacturers inspected supplier parts as they are received. The Continental factory, however, carried this to a degree that was unprecedented. While in a normal production situation a certain number of parts from each shipment would be inspected, many of the shipments received in the Continental plant were one hundred percent inspected. Those inspections that involved only samples involved unusually large ones. Each individual shipment was inspected regardless of the quality of previous shipments from the same supplier. In addition, major parts, such as frames, bodies, and front end sheet metal, were one hundred percent inspected in the suppliers' own plants by resident Continental inspectors prior to shipment. Transmissions were each road tested at the transmission plant and then assembled to their own engines for rigorous dynamometer testing as a unit. Radiators, gas tanks, and glass were all one hundred percent inspected for defects.

4. Additional Manufacturing Attention. The Continental assembly procedures called for approximately twice as many man hours as were used on the Lincoln assembly line. This permitted added operations that were not usually a part of automotive assembly procedures even on high quality cars. The front end sheet metal, for example, was test fitted to the body before painting. This not only insured a proper fit upon final assembly, but also guaranteed a perfect color match. Unusual time and care were given to the entire painting process. It was determined that many mass produced cars were completely assembled in the time it took just to paint a Continental. Each car was also extensively tested for water leaks, for the adjustment of the front end geometry, for wheel balance and for proper tightness of critical bolts. Special emphasis was placed on establishing a quality attitude among employees. No worker was expected to let a defect pass uncorrected even if the item did not fall in the worker's specific area of responsibility. On one occasion cited by Continental executives, a plant guard refused to let a haulaway truck pass through the gates because he noticed a defect in the paint of a car the truck was transporting.

5. In Plant Inspection and Testing. In addition to the quality control procedures already noted, there were fourteen special inspection points strategically placed to monitor quality at important stages of each Mark II's assembly. Each unit was required to pass inspection before being permitted to pass each individual inspection point. As each car was completed it was given an extensive "check out" and road test by a special squad of highly trained mechanics.

6. Top Management Action. A "quality committee" made up of the top management of the Continental Division was established to monitor all phases of the quality control program—inspecting the inspectors. Committee mem-

bers reviewed all statistical information supplied by the quality control department and evaluated results firsthand by frequently driving cars which had been approved for shipment. They also oversaw a weekly inspection of a production car chosen at random by the engineering department, and reviewed in detail customer complaints and repair claims.

7. Field Service. The field service program was established to make sure that any defects that showed up on cars in customer hands were quickly remedied to the customer's satisfaction. In addition to regular dealer service, this program included a number of factory service engineers who traveled around the country personally checking on serious complaints. These service engineers also called on customers who had not reported problems to make sure that they were satisfied with their cars.

Most of the seven steps were also followed in some degree by other manufacturers. The level of commitment in the Continental Division, however, was unprecedented—certainly in the postwar industry.[4]

Upon its introduction, the press was almost embarrassingly enthusiastic about the Mark II. Most of the reports and road tests read as if they were written by Continental Division public relations personnel. *Motor Trend* magazine was typical. A detailed report of the development and design of the Mark II by Executive Editor Don MacDonald had nothing but praise for the car and

1957 Capri.

the concept saying, "We can't help but agree that this kind of approach makes even a $10,000 automobile seem more of a bargain. Our hats are off to a modern classic."[5] In another report in the same issue Editor Walt Woron compared the Mark II to the Rolls-Royce and concluded that it was a worthy successor to the original "Queen of the Classics" Mark I.[6]

The public also liked what it saw, although understandably very few people rushed down to their local Lincoln-Mercury dealer to buy one. Enough did, however, to keep the Continental production line humming throughout the 1956 model year. It was calculated that for the division to break even 1,500 cars would have to be built each year for four years. Production during the initial 1956 model far exceeded that—the final total was 2,556—but the good times were not to last.

Considering that the Lincoln and the Continental Mark II had both been completely new in 1956, it was not expected that there would be very much in the way of changes in 1957. When the 1957 models were announced on Octo-

1957 Continental Mark II convertible by Derham.

ber 16, 1956, however, a surprising number of modifications were in evidence. One of the most interesting, as has been noted, was that the Continental Division had been abolished and the Mark II was now officially a Lincoln product; i.e., a Lincoln in name as well as in fact.

Most of the news, however, was with the standard Lincoln line, the Premieres and Capris. The absence of a four-door hardtop, so sorely felt in the 1956 model year, was remedied. The Premiere and Capri series each had one and the pillared sedans were revised to have a hardtop appearance by virtue of sharing the same roof line. The other most obvious physical difference from the 1956 models was the large and daring canted fins that had sprouted on the rear fenders. The tail lights were, of necessity, revised to fit and the back-up lights were now part of the rear bumper assembly. In design they matched the built-in parking lights of the front bumper assembly, which were enlarged. The front end sheet metal was not changed, but four head lights, or Quadra-Lites, were fitted into the design in an unusual vertical placement. The lower light was a road light and the four could be used all at once or separately in pairs. They were not quad headlights in the modern sense. The side trim was new. There was a more normal rocker panel molding and a thin molding run-

1957 Premiere.

ning the length of the car along the sheet metal crease. The interior was updated with new colors, patterns and fabrics.

The engine was mildly revised. The result was a power increase to 300 horsepower. The dual exhausts, formerly outletting in the rear bumpers, were rerouted to a position beneath the bumper.

The 1957 Lincolns boasted a number of new and improved features and accessories. These included items such as power vent windows, electric door locks and a new six-way power seat. A "Directed-Power" limited-slip differential on other cars and directed the power to whichever rear wheel had the best traction. "Adjust-O-Matic" shock absorbers were available, as was an automatic headlight dimmer control. The "Travel-Tuner" signal seeking radio now included two speakers, an electric antenna and a foot-operated switch which permitted the selection of stations without removing hands from the steering wheel. Seat belts were again listed as an option and, for 1957, a padded instrument panel was finally available. Padded sun visors could also be specified. The air conditioning unit was revised, but still trunk mounted. Power steering and brakes were standard equipment for 1957 and power seats and windows were also standard on Premiere models.

Luxury car sales softened quite a bit in 1957 in anticipation of the 1958 recession. Lincoln faced the additional threats imposed by all-new Cadillac and Imperial lines. Despite this, Lincoln production held up rather well. A total of 41,123 cars were built, including 35,223 Premieres and 5,900 Capris.

The Continental Mark II was not greatly changed for 1957. It shared mechanical alterations with the regular Lincoln lines. The air conditioning intake was relocated so as to eliminate the rear fender cut-outs. Four new metallic exterior colors were available: silver, bronze, medium blue and medium green.

There is considerable dispute over whether a convertible was ever officially offered. Only one was provably built under factory auspices. It was a 1956 model finished in white with a red and white interior. During March, 1957, it was rebuilt to incorporate 1957 design alterations, refinished in metallic blue with a blue and white interior (with black mouton carpeting) and given to Mrs. William Clay Ford. Derham Custom Body Company of Rosemont, Pennsylvania did the original conversion and, according to them, only this one. Although a second one was known to have been privately commissioned and despite the wide publicity given the idea in 1957, the evidence indicated that only one factory-authorized Mark II convertible was actually built.

Continental sales fell precipitously in 1957. Only 444 were built and the car was not continued over into the 1958 model year.

So what happened? Why was the Continental not a success? It has been suggested that the Continental Mark II was too tasteful, too subtle for the expansive era into which it was introduced. It has also been suggested that the market for a $10,000 car simply wasn't as large as Ford thought it was—which would seem to be self-evident, and not really very helpful. It should be noted in this regard that the similarly conceived Cadillac Eldorado Brougham failed to set the world on fire, either. Its impact on the overall market was not much different than that of the Mark II—which is to say negligible—and it was effectively gone after the 1958 model run.[7]

The fundamental problem was that the Special Products team was trying to duplicate the first Continental while ignoring the basic concept behind it. The Mark I was not a car of extraordinary quality or price. Its engineering was rather ordinary and its price was high, but not prohibitively so. The old concept was revived most effectively with the four-seater Thunderbird in 1958

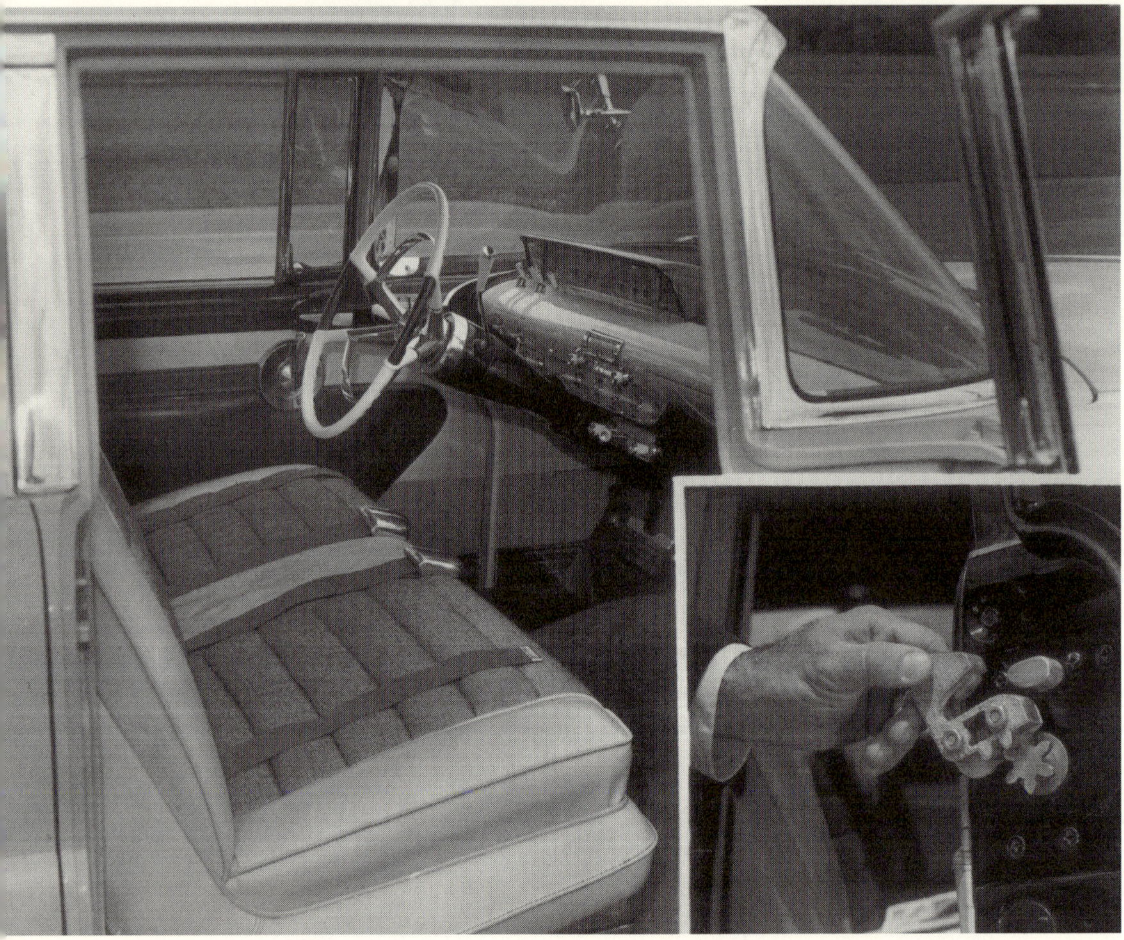

1957 Premiere interior.

and with the Mark III in 1968, in which applications it was remarkably successful. The mistake made with the Mark II was a simple one of overreaching. Like the classic K Lincolns in the late 1930s, the Continental Mark II was splendid but irrelevant for its times.

Yet, if the Continental had been a failure, the standard Lincoln had enjoyed two years of unprecedented success and the company eagerly awaited more of the same with the dramatically new 1958 models.

CHAPTER FIVE

1959 Continental Mark IV.

The Square 'Bird Disaster: 1958–60

THE 1958 LINCOLNS AND CONTINENTALS were under active discussion during most of 1955. It was still intended at that point to retain the Continental as a separate marque with its own distinct body, while Lincoln Division was to continue with the 1956–57 body into the 1958 model year. Plans were being made with that assumption in mind.

In retrospect, it was in the early months of 1956 that the plans began to unravel. The debacle began, curiously, with a decision to build a four-passenger Thunderbird for the 1958 model year. When Robert McNamara—the quintessential bean counter—was named to head the Ford Division in 1955, he ran the numbers and decreed that the car be enlarged to four-seater capacity in order to widen its appeal, and, therefore, potential volume. Confronted with McNamara's decision, Earle MacPherson, the company's chief engineer, insisted that the new T-Bird be built using unibody (frameless) construction—a first for Ford Motor Company.

McNamara was determined to have it his way, as was MacPherson. So a new plant was rushed into planning for a site at Wixom, Michigan, in order to build the car McNamara wanted using the new technology MacPherson wanted. The problem that then arose was that projected Thunderbird volume, even in four-seater form, would not justify the capacity of the new facility. MacPherson's answer to that was to order Lincoln Division to switch its cars to Wixom, as well. Furthermore, since it was impossible to build both unibody and body-and-frame cars on the same assembly line, Lincoln would have to switch, too.

Lincoln Division was immediately thrown into an uproar. Harley Copp, Lincoln's chief engineer, insisted that, a) there wasn't time to do an entirely new Lincoln for 1958, b) there certainly wasn't enough time to do it with a new (to Ford) technology that had never been attempted for a car of the Lincoln's size, and, c) even if it worked unibody technology made annual styling changes far more difficult and expensive, and was, therefore, inappropriate in the luxury segment where being able to respond quickly to market demands was essential. Copp was absolutely correct; the 1958 Lincoln proved to be a disaster for all the reasons noted. (Significantly, Chrysler, which was then planning to switch its entire fleet over to unibody construction by 1960, did not attempt to use it for its Imperial line. The Imperial was roughly equivalent in size and purpose to the Lincoln.)

Worse, the 1958 styling proved no more successful than the engineering. John Najjar was assigned the project and told to make sure the next Lincoln was different from the competition. Najjar decided that Cadillac was into roundness with fins, Chrysler was into wedges, and so staked out Lincoln's turf as being aggressive angularity. Ultimately, the Continental came under

1958 Capri.

his direction, too. The results did not please very many people and Najjar was replaced by Don DeLaRossa when it came time to do the 1959 restyle. DeLaRossa was able to mute much of the design, but the basics were pretty well locked in through the end of the 1960 model run. Actually, these cars were no less tasteful than the Imperials of the period—and arguably better looking than the 1959 Cadillac. Still, it was obvious that massive, aggressive angularity was not the public's fancy.

At any rate, 1958 was supposed to have been the year that Lincoln finally put Cadillac on the run. Everything had been planned for the Great Assault. The Lincoln cars, down to the last bolt, were new and, in some respects, revolutionary. The entirely new Wixom factory incorporated the best and most modern technology for the production of fine cars. The Continental Mark II had been discontinued at the close of the 1957 model run, but its famous name was appropriated for a new top of the line Lincoln series, the Continental Mark III. It was doubtless hoped that the luster of the Continental name would rub off on the new, mainstream Lincolns.

In any case, Lincoln Division finally had Cadillac matched virtually model for model, series for series, in the luxury field, at least with regard to the volume lines. The Capri matched the Cadillac Series Sixty-Two, the Premiere matched the De Ville and the new Continental Mark II matched the Sixty Special sedan. In the highest priced volume class Lincoln even had Cadillac

1958 Continental Mark III.

out-gunned by four models to only one, the Sixty Special. The only Cadillac models not matched were the low-volume Eldorado and the seven-passenger Series Seventy-Five.

The most striking single aspect of the new Lincolns was their physical appearance. They looked enormous. Most of this was a result of highly successful visual deception on the part of Lincoln stylists. While the new models were actually a foot longer than the 1958 Cadillacs, they were only slightly heavier. There certainly was not the vast disparity that people assumed (and continue to assume) existed.

The decision to have a unitized body was made at a time when the state of the technological art had not yet discovered that unitized construction is inefficient in cars beyond a certain size. Lincoln engineers eventually encountered a wide variety of unexpected difficulties stemming from the problem of making a huge frameless vehicle acceptably rigid. One of the reasons for the weight of the production cars was the unusual amount of steel used to reinforce the basic structural integrity of the body. Like the bumblebee, the Lincolns probably shouldn't have been able to fly but did a reasonably good job of it in the end.

1958 engine.

One of the advantages of unitized construction was that it permitted a lower car since the height of the frame did not need to be added to the height of the body. The new Lincolns were, indeed, low, but for all their size were curiously deficient in interior space compared to the old body-and-frame 1957 models. The new models had significantly less head room, front and rear, less front leg room and less front hip room. The 1958 models did excel in shoulder room and in most rear seat dimensions, but the driver and his number one passenger were rather worse off in 1958 than before.

The late 1950s are mostly remembered today for the number and scope of the styling excesses perpetrated by the various manufacturers. Few marques got through the era without producing at least one or two models whose styling suffers in retrospect, and the styling of the 1958–1960 Lincolns is not fondly remembered by many. It is important to understand that it looked better within the context of its own time. In a sense you had to be there to appreciate why these cars seemed so much more attractive to people actually living at the time. No less an artist than Norman Rockwell was induced to endorse the Lincoln, as were a number of other Americans of presumed culture.

The new Lincoln "look" began at the front end with radically canted headlights surrounding a recessed grille. The texture of the grille was similar to that on 1957 Lincoln and Continental models, respectively. Beneath the grille was a huge sculptured bumper with double-canted fins on either side. The peak in the headlight surrounds extended along the fenders to the rear of the car where it ended in smallish, canted tail fins. Lincolns had single light units on either side of the rear end, while Continentals had three on either side, for a total of six. These light clusters included tail lights, stop lights, back-up lights and directional signals. The rear had its own massive bumper below the lights and a thick chrome molding above them forming a large oval area around the lights. This area had its own grille texture similar to that in front. The gas tank filler pipe was concealed behind the center of the rear grille.

The sides used very little chrome trim but did sport elaborately sculptured areas around the front and rear wheel cut-outs. The greenhouse had a peculiar appearance. Part of this was due to the way it sat, nestled between the pontoon-like full-length fender line. This perhaps more than anything else, was what made the cars look so large. The rear window was a wrap-around affair on Lincolns. On Continentals, it assumed an unprecedented reverse slant and the center portion retracted. This was even true of the Continental convertible. The convertible also used a flashy two-tone top which disappeared completely from sight beneath a hinged steel deck panel.

The interior trim was entirely redesigned for 1958, and made use of four basic design motifs and eleven different fabrics in addition to vinyl and Bridge of Weir Scottish leather. The instrument panel, which had followed one basic design since the 1950 models, was completely redone. The instruments were now clustered together in a single pod placed directly in front of the driver. Standard safety features included the deep-dish steering wheel, a padded instrument panel, padded sun visors and dual speed windshield wipers. For added safety, the power windows could be had with a lock-out feature at extra cost. Power window switches were built into the door arm rests. The arm rests not only functioned as control panels, but also concealed the rear seat heater ducts. For the first time, the air conditioning unit was mounted in the engine compartment.

Air suspension was planned as an option on the 1958 models and the body was designed to accept it. Early publicity indicated that it would follow soon after the new model announcement. Lincoln engineers, however, experienced sufficient problems that it was eventually discarded. At that, they were more fortunate than their opposite numbers at General Motors. GM gave air suspension a big push in the 1958–59 period and had nothing but grief to show for it.

The four-way power seat and remote control rear view mirror (on the driver's side) continued to be standard equipment on all Lincolns. A new standard feature was the electric antenna.

The new models had a new 430 cubic inch engine, which, in some form, was shared with both Mercury and Edsel. It delivered 375 horsepower. The compression ratio was now up to 10.5 to 1. The engine featured a new block, a stronger crankshaft, heavier connecting rods and improved lubrication and cooling. The combustion chamber had a wedge shape to increase the turbulence of the fuel mixture and provide better burning.

The Turbo-Drive transmission was redesigned to handle the greater engine power. Brakes were made 44 percent bigger to handle the increased vehicle weight. Coil springs were featured all around with trailing arms in the rear.

Ten models were available in the various Lincoln lines. A pillared sedan, four-door sedan and a two-door hardtop were featured on all three lines, while the convertible was available only as a Continental.

The press was almost uniformly enthusiastic about the new models at the time of their introduction in the fall of 1957. One of the recurrent themes of contemporary reports was that these were fast cars with tremendous performance capabilities. This is entirely contrary to the popular view of them today as having been fat, wallowing barges.

Joe Wherry, writing in *Motor Trend*, said:

> From behind the wheel the driver is immediately aware that he's in a huge car. The illusion of obesity is, however, quickly dispelled when you place the lever-operated transmission control in DRIVE position and mash the throttle. For a car weighing right at 5,000 pounds you are surprised to zoom to a true 60 mph in 19.9 seconds . . . in the handling department, this rig will stack up with the finest anywhere in the big limousine class . . . Will Lincoln improve its position? I think there's no doubt but what this whopper car will make terrific gains.[1]

Owners of the new Lincolns, unfortunately, were not quite so entranced. An indepth survey of 1958 Lincoln, Cadillac and Imperial owners was run by *Popular Mechanics* late in the model year, and the results, at least insofar as the Lincoln was concerned, were disturbing. Lincoln had by far the lowest approval rating of the three marques, and a substantial 16.9 percent of those responding called their cars "poor." This was three-and-a-half times the Imperial disapproval figure and nearly nine-and-a-half times that of Cadillac. Almost half the Cadillac owners had no complaints of any kind with their cars, but only one out of four Lincoln owners could say the same thing.

Serious Lincoln complaints included poor workmanship (29.3 percent), body rattles and squeaks (17.7 percent), engine noise and troubles (15.8 percent) and radio antenna trouble (14.0 percent). Nearly one out of three Lincoln owners reported some trouble with the engine and nearly one out of five reported considerable trouble. Less than half the Lincoln owners said they

1958 Premiere.

would buy another (48.8 percent) while the corresponding Imperial and Cadillac figures were 51.2 percent and 75.9 percent, respectively.

The obvious conclusion from all this was that the new Lincolns were simply not as satisfactory to their owners as the 1958 Cadillacs and Imperials. Considering Lincoln Division's proclaimed emphasis on quality with the 1958 cars, the high number of quality related complaints represented a severe failure.

The 1958 recession hurt all manufacturers except American Motors, and Lincoln suffered too. The sad news, however, was that, despite entirely new models in which Lincoln executives had placed so much hope, they actually lost ground against their arch-rival. Cadillac, with a warmed over car, was off 17 percent, but Lincoln production was down a startling 38.5 percent. Only 29,684 cars were built, including 6,859 Capris, 19,275 Premieres and 12,550 Continentals.

After the incredible exertions surrounding the development and birth of the 1958 models little that was new was expected for 1959. The most interesting development was administrative. The Lincoln Division was merged into the conglomerate M-E-L Division in January, 1959.[2] The M-E-L Division encompassed Mercury, Edsel and Lincoln operations as well as foreign Ford products being imported into the United States. It was billed as a great advance, but obviously was necessitated by the declining fortunes of the Edsel and Lincoln brands. Separate administrative staffs on the General Motors plan could no longer be justified without the sort of volume production General Motors had achieved in the medium and luxury price classes.

So, by the time the 1959 Lincolns and Continentals were announced to the public it had become all too clear that they had failed in their prime objective: establishing Lincoln in a commanding position in the luxury car field. It was not anticipated that much could be done about this in 1959. Salvation would have to await the next major body change scheduled for 1961. In the meantime, the quality control problems that had plagued the early 1958 models were corrected. Weld efficiency, so critical in a unitized body, and which had been running at 60–75 percent, was raised by concerted effort to 90–95 percent. Additional noise dampening was done around the transmission and drive shaft to cure problems in that area.

The models were mildly restyled. Most of the alterations occurred in the front end. The deeply recessed grille, probably the least attractive single feature of the 1958 design, was substantially modified. The grille was moved forward a bit and now blended into the area around the canted headlights. The front bumper was redesigned to lessen the effect of the double-canted fins on the ends. The fins were given bullet-shaped protrusions containing the parking lights. It made for a cleaner, more normal sort of frontal appearance. The exaggerated front quarter panel sculpturing of the 1958 models, which some wags had labeled "pre-dented," was toned down and extended back into the front door panels. The rear end design was altered only slightly. The whole car took on a crisper, leaner look.

The cars were mechanically the same as before with only a few minor exceptions. The compression ratio of the engine, for example, was reduced slightly to 10.0 to 1. This resulted in a horsepower decrease from 375 to 350.

This line-up was mostly the same, too. The Capri name, however, was discarded. Once again, as in 1955, the base series had no designation. It was simply a Lincoln. The Lincoln Premiere series remained unchanged as did the Continental, now promoted to "Mark IV."

The Mark IV did have a couple of new models, though, in the semi-custom town car and limousine. The hand of James Nance, M-E-L's general manager was obvious. Unable to fund limousine models at Lincoln, he took the same route he had when he was running Packard a few years earlier: hiring an outside conversion house to prepare a small run of modified production cars.

Thus, the town car and limousine were little more than modified Continental four-door sedans. The roof was redone in a formal style with a black, padded top and a smaller rear window. The limousine had a partition inside, but otherwise both cars used stock Continental interior trim. The conversion

1959 Continental Mark IV.

work was done by Hess & Eisenhardt in Cincinnati to Lincoln specifications. These cars were mounted on the standard 131 inch wheelbase and were still six passenger vehicles. Very few were built.

If 1958 was the year Lincoln failed to challenge Cadillac for supremacy in the luxury car field, 1959 was the year Lincoln fell even further behind. The industry as a whole was doing much better in 1959 after having some real nightmares during the 1958 recession. Cadillac, despite introducing the most garish new models in its history, produced 17 percent more cars in the 1959 model year than they had during 1958. Lincoln production, in contrast, declined by 9 percent even over 1958's depressed (and depressing) totals, and the gap between it and Cadillac widened still more. Final production for the 1959 run was 26,906, the lowest figure since the abbreviated 1948 model run. Of these, 11,126 were Continentals, 7,851 were Premieres, and 7,929 were standard Lincolns. The Continental total included 49 limousines and 78 town cars.

1959 Continental Mark IV Town Limousine.

The 1960 range included a greater number of modifications on the 1958–1959 design than is generally realized. The cars were not radically different, but a fair amount of money was spent on them.

The four-barrel carburetor was dropped in favor of a two-barrel job. This caused the horsepower to make a sharp decline to 315. Although the interesting automatic lubrication system—the press of a button on the instrument panel lubed the entire front end—had never been standard equipment, it was deleted from the accessory catalog after 1960. The rest of the changes in the cars were visual.

The front end styling was completely done over again. The finned bumpers were gone for good, and in their stead were fairly ordinary wrap-around bumpers sporting dagmar-type bumper guards reminiscent of those used on the 1954–55 Lincolns. Headlights were still canted, but the bumper dipped down in the middle to allow for a much larger grille area than before. Lincoln and Continental models still retained their own distinctive grille textures which were, as in years past, repeated on the smaller grilles surrounding the tail lights. The rear end was also completely done over. The old oval grille area between the deck lid and the massive rear bumper was now squared off. The canted fins were the same, but for 1960 they extended boldly down into the rear grille area. This served to call attention to them at a time when other manufacturers were trying to hide their fins, but, then, this particular Lincoln body never had been in fashion, anyway, so it was a moot point.

The roof design of the Lincolns was new. It no longer had the Continental style of reversed angle at the back window. The actual windows on the Lincolns had never had the Continental reverse slant, but now the roof sheet metal didn't either. Side trim was slightly modified on both lines and the front and rear quarter panels were revised just enough to accommodate the front and rear restylings. The 1960 models were definitely crisper and more normal in appearance than before, but without losing their Lincoln "look."

The interiors were restyled, as well. The main new feature was the instrument panel pod in front of the driver. There were now four large circular housings on top of the pod containing most of the important gauges, as well as the ventilator-heater-air conditioning control which was still operated with one dial.

Tom McCahill, the dean of American automotive writers, reviewed all of the 1960 cars for True's Automobile Yearbook and had a few choice words about the 1960 Lincolns:

> Lincoln . . . has not undergone too many obvious changes for 1960. The styling has gone very boxy, and it is very hard for this writer to remember that

back in '56 and '57 Lincolns were among the best-looking cars on the road (anyhow, in '56 they were the best-looking car, regardless). This is something I feel sure they will not be accused of in 1960. For 1960 they have replaced the former four-barrel carburetor with a two-barrel job—which is an interesting switch—sort of like Charlie Atlas coming out against muscles.

The model line-up was unchanged for 1960. Final production came to 24,820 units, down almost 8 percent from 1959's miserable totals. Of these,

Top, 1960 Continental Mark V; *bottom*, 1960 Continental Mark V interior.

11,086 were Continental Mark Vs, 6,574 were Lincoln Premieres, and 7,160 were Lincolns. Exactly 170 Hess & Eisenhardt conversions were done on the Continental body that year, including 34 limousines and 136 town cars.

This was the last year for this particular Lincoln body. Ford executives could probably hardly wait for it to be over and done with. The 1958–1960 Lincolns and Continentals were, in their own way, as big a disappointment as the Edsel. What the Edsel was supposed to have done for the corporation's penetration of the medium price class the Lincolns and Continentals were supposed to have done with the luxury field. Their failure was less only to the extent that the Lincoln nameplate managed to survive the fiasco. In three years Lincoln had lost exactly half its market penetration, and Cadillac, the great rival, was further out of reach than ever.

The public must have been increasingly bewildered, by this juncture, at the constant twists and turns in Lincoln's marketing strategy. Unlike Cadillac, which put great emphasis on continuity and often seemed to be able to make the most radical changes while seeming to remain the same, Lincoln came across as being erratic. The 1949, 1952, 1956 and 1958 Lincolns could have been built by four different car companies. They were all good cars in most ways, and even possessed touches of brilliance, but the public was getting less and less sure of just what a Lincoln was supposed to be. And Lincoln management—which was not sure, either—was hardly in a position to tell them.

Lincoln had entered the decade building 9 percent of the luxury cars sold in America. After ten years of frantic activity, that figure stood at 11 percent—and was on the decline. What Lincoln had desperately needed all along was a coherent, long-term strategy. Periodic, unrelated, short-term efforts clearly had not done the trick.

The 1958–1960 Lincolns and Continentals were not bad cars. They were, in fact, far better than they are remembered as having been. Most of the important automotive writers raved about them when they first appeared on the scene, but they certainly bombed at the box office, and those are the only reviews that count in the end.

CHAPTER SIX

1961 Continental.

Lincoln Finds Its Voice: 1961–65

THE TEPID PUBLIC RECEPTION accorded the 1958 Lincolns and Continentals was a real shock to those men charged with guiding Lincoln's fortunes. Everything had been done to insure a dramatic success. These were the cars that were certain to catapult Lincoln to the top of the luxury market once and for all . . . only something closer to the reverse actually happened. The 1958 models lost ground over the competition, and Lincoln's decline in market penetration picked up frightening momentum in 1959 and 1960. The first model year of the 1960s saw Lincoln almost back to where it had been ten years before. It was as if an entire decade of frenetic activity, and the expenditure of untold tens of millions of dollars, had amounted to nothing.

Something akin to the American post-Vietnam War psychosis began to set in around the executive offices of the Ford Motor Company. Normally self-assured men began to ask themselves why everything seemed to have gone wrong, and why did they not see it coming, and what could they do about it now? The Lincoln's decline was certainly not due to timid management. Neither effort nor dollars had been spared. Clearly, something more fundamental was involved.

Eugene Bordinat, by that time director of the Lincoln styling studio, thought he knew where to find the answer Lincoln so urgently needed. While Lincoln had been flailing around, a certain other luxury brand had been advancing from strength to strength. What, Bordinat asked, had Cadillac done that Lincoln hadn't? Cadillacs had not been better or prettier, on average. The Cadillac advantage, he concluded, lay in its continuity. Cadillac was using the same series designations it had used since before World War II. Its basic grille textures had not varied since the early 1930s. Its fins had been a constant since the late 1940s. In short, no matter how much body or engineering changes had altered the substance of the cars, they had always looked like Cadillacs. Even the monstrous 1959 models, sort of a theater of the absurd on wheels, had met with broad public acceptance. It may have represented the final bankruptcy of the tail fin concept, it may have reached the point of self-caricature, but it produced almost five times as many sales as the (comparatively) tasteful 1959 Lincoln.

From this, Bordinat became convinced that for Lincoln to succeed it would have to establish a single, coherent identity and then stick with it over a period of years. For want of a better place to start, Bordinat began working up a 1961 proposal carrying forward the basic design themes embodied in the 1958–60 cars. Don DeLaRossa, who had restyled the 1959 and 1960s cars, worked with him. Meanwhile, Special Products was working on a completely unrelated design for a proposed 1961 Thunderbird. This seemingly unrelated design project was to have an unexpected and dramatic influence upon Lincoln history.

Although George Walker had been in control of most of the styling at Ford Motor Company since his design proposal for the 1949 Ford was accepted in 1946, he had remained an outside consultant until 1955. In May of that year, he was named vice-president in charge of styling. One of the men he brought with him to Ford was Elwood P. Engel. Engel had been assigned to Special Products, and in August, 1958, he had just finished an assignment to develop a new Thunderbird in the Mark II tradition. The result was stunning. Robert S. McNamara, then in charge of overall automotive operations, chanced upon it one day and asked Engel to turn it into a Lincoln. In two weeks, the Thunderbird was stretched into a Lincoln four-door sedan. When management saw it, they bought it "hook, line and sinker" (according to Engel),[1] and, in fact, the 1961 Lincoln Continental was produced almost verbatim from this initial two-week wonder.

The continuity that Bordinat rightly wanted for Lincoln would have to start in 1961, rather than in 1958, it seemed. He and his team cannot be faulted for attempting to develop the 1958-60 design into an acceptable 1961 proposal, but the Engel product was so dramatically superior that it commanded attention.

So, Bordinat and DeLaRossa set to work with Engel to bring the proposal to production status. They joined Engel's assistants, John Najjar, Robert M. Thomas and Colin G. Neale. Harold C. MacDonald was the project's chief engineer.

The 1960 drive-train was, for the most part, carried over for 1961. The unibody construction was also retained—and improved. The car required unibody construction due to its height, but its sales couldn't support the entire facility unaided. The Lincoln and the Thunderbird together made the plant sustainable, so body and frame construction was never a serious option for the 1961 Lincoln. Some sharing of components was even arranged: both cars used the same basic cowl structure, for example.

The 1961 Lincoln Continental was something no Lincoln had been since the original Continental: it was influential. Lincoln had made all sorts of cars since the war. Some sold well and some didn't, some were exciting and some weren't, but none of them had sent the competition rushing to its drawing boards in the great Detroit game of "catch up." Until 1961, Lincoln had always been the one playing from behind. Now, suddenly, Cadillac and Imperial were eating Lincoln's dust. The 1961 Lincoln Continental, in fact, sparked a styling revolution in Detroit that was felt far outside the luxury car field and which continues even to this day. The influence on Cadillac styling was seen as early as 1963, but Chrysler paid the ultimate compliment: it hired Engel away from Ford. If the 1964 Imperial was not exactly a Lincoln clone, it was obviously cut from similar cloth.

The actual sales of the 1961 Lincoln Continental were a mild disappointment to management, even though they were definitely up in a market that was decidedly down. They undoubtedly would have risen more if the line had included any two-door models. The important thing was that the momentum was finally going in the right direction. Management, determined to stick with a winner, made few meaningful changes in the original Engel design until the 1966 model year.

Market evaluations begun in 1963 under the direction of William Clay Ford explored ways in which Lincoln might improve its market share. It was discovered that the addition of a coupe to the line combined with a more competitive pricing policy was the way to go. It was also discovered that the Continental's slow sales curve was deceptive. Owner satisfaction was up so dramatically that it had produced a serious decline in trade-ins. The corollary was that the number of "captive" sales, i.e., the number of Cadillac and Imperial owners switching over, was increasing. Both trends were fine omens for the future, even though the first did serve to restrain sales in the short run.

The use of the name "Lincoln Continental" was made partly to indicate a merging of the two separate Lincoln and Continental lines, and partly to evoke memories of the earlier Continental Marks I & II. (The Marks III through V were all but disowned by the company, and in later years as subsequent cars were redesignated as "Marks" beginning with the Mark III in 1968. The automobile industry would seem to have something in common with the sports world: they only retire your number if they like you!)

The similarities between the 1961 Lincoln Continentals and the Marks I and II were more than just advertising verbiage. All three cars were consummate examples of good taste, and recognized as such even in their own era. All three cars were successful advocates of the less-is-more school of automotive design. Indeed, the subtlety of the Mark II was quite probably one of the causes of its untimely demise. The public was not ready for understated sophistication in 1956.

Several of the styling themes of the 1961 Lincoln Continentals were carried over from the Mark II, as well. The tail light design was similar. The belt molding used a small rise just ahead of the rear wheel cut-out much like the fender crease on the Mark II. The roof lines, especially at the back, were close, and although the grille design was not created specifically for the 1961 Lincoln Continental—it was just something they had lying around the styling studio at the time—it did employ a typical Mark II mesh texture. The back-hinged, suicide rear doors also harkened back to the classic era of which the Mark I was the culmination. (The company called them "clam shell" doors.)

The first impression people had of the 1961 models was of their sparing use of chrome trim. The sides were virtually bare, and the design as a whole was exceedingly simple and elegant. The only feature that seemed even slightly "busy" to the early reviewers was the small grille above the rear bumper, one of the few themes carried over from the 1960 design. As before, it repeated the front grille texture and hid the gas tank filler pipe. The center-opening doors were dictated by the abbreviated wheelbase of the new models, down eight inches from 1960. Rear doors could not be made wide enough to allow sufficient room for passenger entry and exit without hinging them at the back.

This feature would have been sufficiently novel on a sedan, but having a similar convertible model in the line was genuinely radical. The decision was made to stick with unibody construction because of the fantastic investment in unibody machinery at the Wixom plant, and, yet, Ford and Lincoln-Mercury officials were not enthusiastic about putting too much cash into another new Lincoln, so they hit upon the idea of a convertible sedan. This was the first American four-door convertible since the 1951 Frazer.

Lincoln unibody experience had improved substantially since the 1958 models, and the new bodies were 67 percent more torsionally rigid than the old and among the most rigid bodies in the industry. The bodies were so rigid, in fact, that the convertibles did not require any kind of special "beefing up," something highly unusual for an open car. The convertibles were about 300 pounds heavier than the sedans, but 200 pounds of this was due to the added weight

Top, the 1961 presidential parade car in which John F. Kennedy was killed in 1963; *bottom*, production version of the 1961 Continental.

of the convertible top mechanism. The top retracted into the trunk area, much as the 1957–59 Ford retractables had done, with the rear deck lid being hinged in the back. It played havoc with trunk space, but kept the top out of sight and permitted decent room in the passenger compartment.

The other 100 pounds of weight in the convertibles was due to tuning weights positioned at the four corners of the car to cancel out harmonic vibrations at speeds between 51 and 62 miles an hour. One other feature: the rear door windows automatically retracted 4-1/2 inches when the rear doors were opened to prevent binding.

A few other body features were worthy of note. These were the first Lincolns in several years to eliminate the "dog-leg" wrap-around windshield that became such a fad in the late 1950s. The side glass was curved, the first time this had been done on a Lincoln. It allowed for more shoulder room and also led to the inward-sloping greenhouse. The resultant "teepee" effect was made all the more noticeable by an unusually high beltline, another styling theme borrowed from the late, unlamented 1958–1960 bodies. The greenhouse seemed to be cradled between the fenders. The beltline also had a full-length

1961 Continental.

molding running from the top of the front bumper all the way back to the top of the tail lights. This was the first time that had been done, and caused quite a bit of comment.

The 1961 models were substantially more compact than the models they replaced. They were shorter by 8 inches in wheelbase and 14.8 inches in length, lower by 3.3 inches and narrower by 1.7 inches. Oddly enough, they were not much lighter. The 1961 sedan weighed a scant 90 pounds less than its 1960 counterpart. This, perhaps better than any other statistic, gives testimony to the limitations of the unibody art of the area as it applied to large cars. The new models were reasonably space efficient, leg room remained virtually the same as before and head room was within a few tenths of an inch, but the volume of interior space was noticeably less than in 1960.

Interiors were styled in the same good taste that characterized the exterior appearance. The instrument panel was completely redesigned and divided into three areas. The instruments and gauges were located in a recessed area at the left, and a matching area on the right contained the glove box. A fully transistorized radio was positioned in the middle. The air conditioning con-

1961 Continental interior.

trols and outlets, if ordered at extra cost, pulled down from a panel immediately below the radio. Real wood could be specified, as well, for the instrument panel and the doors. The standard finish was aluminum. Twenty-one solid colors were available, but two-tone exterior colors were not offered.

A special feature of the instrument panel was the gauge cluster. This was done in the Continental truncated diamond motif. Instruments included a "door ajar" warning light. It may have been a first in the industry, and was a real necessity in a car with suicide rear doors.

The 430 cubic inch engine, still the largest in the industry in displacement, was carried over from 1960. It was now a Lincoln exclusive, though. Some effort was made to reduce its height, but it and the rest of the drive-train were essentially unchanged from 1960.

New hydraulic windshield wipers, in an unusual arrangement, worked off the power steering pump which was placed directly ahead of the engine so that it, in turn, could work off the crankshaft. The front drum brakes on convertibles used flared aluminum shells with cast iron inserts. Braking effort was supposed to have been reduced by 20 percent, steering effort by 25 percent. In order to finally beat the noise problems that had plagued the previous unitized bodies, tremendous work was done to perfect sound-deadening around the underbody, and the drive train rode on heavy rubber bushings especially developed to absorb road shock and noise.

Additional effort was expended to raise the general level of quality to new heights, even, perhaps especially, in the little details. The parking brake cable was given a nylon inner liner to fight rust and corrosion. Rocker panels were galvanized and the lower 18 inches of each body was dipped into a rust-proofing solution. The electric window motors were sealed in liquid rubber and had stainless steel shafts. All instrument panel wiring was nylon coated.

The new Lincoln Continentals were put through the most stringent testing procedures in modern times. Each engine was "hot" tested for three hours, then torn down for a visual inspection before reassembly and installation. A computer-like electronic device checked every electrical component. All generators were likewise pre-tested. Each car received a three-minute water spray test. To check for lubrication leaks, each car was supplied with a special fluorescent dye and observed under a black light. Finally, each car was run through a grueling twelve-mile road test by a specially trained mechanic whose job was to find fault with it. There were sixteen such men.

The road test actually began with a check of the brakes, transmission, and steering on a half-mile long test track at the Wixom plant. Following this, the car left the plant grounds for its twelve-mile drive through the Michigan countryside in a route encompassing not only winding rural roads but also stretches of modern superhighways. Every working system was checked, including the smallest details.

Even cigarette lighters did not escape scrutiny. Each lighter was tested for the amount of pressure required to engage it, how long it took to pop back out, and the quality of the sound as it popped—audible, but not objectionable.

Each driver would go through each car in this fashion methodically checking 189 items for the quality of their function and adjustment. Any unsatisfactory items were then corrected and retested until they passed inspection. The entire testing procedure normally took about one-and-a-half hours.

The elaborate care with which each Lincoln Continental was built prompted the factory to take one of its most notable steps: the two-year/24,000 mile warranty. This was a time when the typical new car warranty was 90 days/3,000 miles. The ensuing publicity—and there was quite a bit of it—worked much to the Lincoln Continental's advantage, as did the advertised 6,000 mile oil change and 30,000 mile lubrication intervals.

Press reaction to the new Lincoln Continentals was uniformly favorable. *Motor Trend* was typical in a road test that appeared in the April, 1961, issue. They praised the styling, calling it "one of the most distinctive in any luxury car," and lamented that the exceptional appearance of the new Lincolns might distract attention from other noteworthy features. One major complaint voiced concerned the seats, which *Motor Trend* testers found to be lacking in sufficient support for long trips. On the other hand, they found the same seats to be exceptionally comfortable in local driving.

Motor Trend did credit the new Continentals with starting a couple of important new industry trends:

> The most significant trend in the luxury class is...one of size and body styles. The most dramatic change is in the new Lincoln Continental, which is 15 inches shorter this year...Although not so pronounced, the trend in few body styles is becoming apparent. Lincoln Continental is also the most dramatic, with its drop to two different styles.

Car Life was ecstatic about the new Lincolns, especially regarding the styling which, according to their report, "scores mightily" and also rated the quality "second to none."[2] The new Lincolns eventually received the *Car Life* 1961 Engineering Excellence Award. In summation of their reasons for their selection they wrote, "Here is a car extraordinary—one that is designed to be beautiful and comfortable, and built to be long-lived and reliable."[3]

Once again, the Industrial Designers' Institute saw fit to present one of its coveted awards to an automobile manufacturer, this time for the 1961 Lincoln

Continental. This was the second time a Lincoln had won the I.D.I. award, the first being in 1956 in recognition of the Lincoln Premiere hardtop.

That the 1961 Lincoln Continental represented an achievement of tremendous stature cannot be doubted, certainly not in retrospect. Curiously, the new models seemed to have been a mild disappointment to Ford officials (it was Lincoln-Mercury Division once again, the Edsel having been dropped in fact as well as in name).

Several factors undoubtedly acted to restrain sales. The year was not a good one for the industry as a whole. Nearly every manufacturer reported a decline in production over the previous year's totals, including Cadillac—and Cadillac had introduced a new line of cars of its own for 1961. Lincoln no longer had a complete range of models. There was no two-door hardtop, a lapse which had to have hurt, and while no one else had a four-door convertible, not many buyers wanted one. It was a novelty, and even Lincoln-Mercury officials would have preferred a two-door convertible instead—if they could have afforded it.

Against all this, however, Lincoln scored rather well with a slight (1.3 percent) increase in production for the model run. What no one could see at the time, of course, was that this was the beginning of Lincoln's slow, steady rise as a luxury car producer. There was going to be little but good news ahead.

Production for the 1961 model year totaled 25,164 units. Of these 22,307 were sedans and 2,857 were convertibles. There is some question as to whether any four-door hardtops were built. Some factory data suggests that four such cars may have been produced, but there is no confirmation. At least one hardtop exists in the form of a photograph, but whether the car itself was a production model or simply a prototype is impossible to determine. Certainly, it would have been a relatively simple task to build a four-door hardtop—all the parts existed already between the two standard Lincoln Continental models—so simple, in fact, that one is tempted to ask why one was not included in the model line-up. Research has not yet turned up the answer to that intriguing question.

Without question, the most famous 1961 Continental was the stretched parade car delivered to the Secret Service in the spring of 1961. It was also the most elaborate to date, although, as events would prove, not elaborate enough. Converted by Hess & Eisenhardt in Cincinnati, this car was destined to be the one in which President John F. Kennedy was assassinated in Dallas, Texas, in November, 1963.

At 7,822 pounds, it was the second heaviest presidential car up to that time, exceeded only by the armor-plated 1939 Sunshine Special. It was 33 inches longer than the production Continental, and included an array of gadgetry previously unknown. According to one account, the President's car could "pop him up and down, footlight him, air condition him, and let him sit in a top hat beneath any three different roofs." Actually, there were only two different roofs for the rear compartment: a limousine style roof and a bubbletop. The third roof was a detachable section for the front compartment.

Step plates were built into the rear bumper on either side of a huge continental tire, with grip handles that retracted into the rear deck. Twin spot lights as well as running lights were located up front. The age of television had its effect on the cars: it was painted a special dark metallic blue so that it would appear to be the popular sort of shiny black at night under the television lights that were now a normal part of all public functions.

The bubbletop, incidentally, was fashioned from ordinary Plexiglas and was by no means bulletproof. To that extent, its use could not have prevented the president's death. The real error in Dallas was in declining permission for Secret Service agents to be positioned on the rear step plates during the motorcade. The Service remains convinced that an agent stationed on the right-hand step plate would have completely blocked the line of sight between the school Book Depository Building from which the fatal shots were fired and the president seated on the right side of the car's rear compartment.

In any case, Dallas forced a complete rethinking of presidential security measures. Secret Service techniques were revised and refined, and the cars, too, were destined to be much different in coming years. The Kennedy car was returned to Hess & Eisenhardt in 1964 for a major overhaul. By the time it was returned to the Secret Service in June, 1964, it had been almost completely rebuilt.[4]

But that was all in the future. For 1962, the production models were not greatly changed. Still, there were numerous alterations and refinements, and quite a bit more than most people realize. The basic car, however, remained the same and the fact that there was no effort made to have it "look" different was a novelty in itself. The annual model change had become such a ritual by this time throughout the industry that Lincoln's refusal to play the game was as newsworthy as a facelift would have been (and a whole lot less expensive). The position expressed by Lincoln-Mercury officials was that they had a winner, so why mess with it? This notion was to have considerable influence on industry thinking. Ben D. Mills, general manager of Lincoln-Mercury Division, stated the company's philosophy at the time of the 1962 model announcement:

> Change for the sake of change will not be characteristic of this luxury automobile. Instead of a different looking car each year, our goal is to make changes which will help us build as perfect a luxury automobile as possible.[5]

The physical appearance changes in the 1962 models were of the most minor nature, and most occurred in the area around the grille. The texture was changed from the familiar Continental mesh-type to a series of small rectangles. This pattern was repeated in the small grille area below the rear deck lid. Headlights were positioned an inch higher than before and the center impact bar that had divided the grille horizontally on 1961 models was deleted. It was felt by stylists that the grille "was not readable from a distance, due to the light reflection angle of the lower area." Such are the daily concerns of people in the Motor City. In any case, a thin bar now ran horizontally across the center of the grille to give it some extra definition, but not so much that people would be distracted.

Inside, the quality of the vinyl upholstery was improved and, for the first time, seat belt anchors were fitted on all cars and the belts themselves were

1962 Continental interior.

once again available from the factory. Other new options included remote control outside mirrors, an automatic headlight dimmer, an automatic rear deck release, an electric antenna and power vent windows.

Quite a number of quality improvements were made. The sheer metal joints on top of the instrument panel were revised for a more finished look. A new door lock design permitted 50 percent less key effort than before. The appearance of the luggage compartment was improved with better lining material. Body insulation was improved by the use of 33 percent heavier felt sound deadener for the floor panel and firewall areas and so on. Ford was determined not to rest on its laurels with the new Continental.

Production in 1962 rose by better than 23 percent for a final total of 31,061 units. This was a greater increase than the other luxury car makers could claim and offered further proof of the solid acceptance of the new Lincoln Continental style and philosophy. As in 1961, the overwhelming majority of the cars built were sedans; only 3,212 four-door convertibles were produced.

The 1963 models continued the Lincoln Continental practice of styling continuity with changes made in order that the new models might be improved, not merely different. Visual changes, however, were more readily apparent than those in the 1962 models. The biggest change, figuratively and literally, was the redesigned rear deck lid. It was higher and more boxy. That together with a complete redesign of the trunk area resulted in a substantial improvement in trunk space. The Continental, which had suffered along with one of the smallest trunks in the industry, suddenly had one of the largest. The rear grille was also modified with a new "vertical theme" and a bolder molding surrounding it. The vertical theme consisted of eight stylized Continental stars running side-to-side across the width of the grille.

The interior was not greatly changed, either. Engineers were able to get a bit more rear leg room and front knee room out of the same space, and the instrument panel was slightly revised. An AM-FM radio was listed in the accessories catalogue for the first time.

There were numerous mechanical modifications for 1963. Sedans now used the flared aluminum brake drums that had previously been available only on the convertibles. All models were equipped with alternators, easing battery drain and permitting power generation at low speeds, or even at idle.

The 1963 version of Lincoln's 430 cubic inch engine had a four-barrel carburetor once again (it had been dropped in favor of a two-barrel in 1960). A unique new manifold was designed to handle it. The carburetor was positioned so that the primary barrels were centered on the manifold, rather than centering the entire carburetor, on the reasoning that the primaries would be

1963 Continental.

used 90 percent of the time and superior fuel distribution could thus be had under most circumstances. The compression ratio was increased to 10.1 to 1. Horsepower, too, was increased to 320. Gas mileage, however, suffered somewhat. The 1963 models turned in mileage figures in the 9–14 miles per gallon range, down approximately one mile per gallon from 1962.

Motor Trend magazine tested a Continental sedan once again in 1963 and liked it even better than they had in 1961, commenting:

> You really appreciate the term luxury as it's so aptly applied to a car like the Lincoln Continental . . . On long, open-road trips you really know you're in a luxury car. Wind and road noises are most noticeable by their almost complete absence . . . This is the result of some extensive engineering on Lincoln's part in the areas of sound-deadening materials and where and how to use them. Coupled with their equally extensive work in the field of chassis tuning (as it applies to shake and vibration frequencies), the result is a car that's as solid and free from vibrations and noises as any car on the road, bar none . . . Interior and exterior detailing in the Continental is above reproach. Everything fits as it should and only the highest-quality upholstery and carpeting materials are used . . . While the price of the Continental is fairly high, it has a list of standard equipment that would run at least $1,000 if bought separately . . . Add these to the Continental's other qualities and the obvious answer is that the Lincoln buyer gets an awful lot of value for his money.[6]

Ben Mills couldn't have said it better himself.

Lincoln maintained its market position in 1963 as production edged up a hair to 31,233, including 28,095 sedans and 3,138 convertibles.

The 1964 Lincoln Continental incorporated the largest number of important changes of any model since 1961. While retaining the basic styling themes of previous models, it refined and revised them in an evolutionary way and included a few new features that materially improved the final product.

The grille, which is usually the first thing the stylists attack when they are facelifting a car, was actually the least of the alterations. The subtle vertical bars of the 1963 design were boldened considerably, and the dip in the upper grille molding was deleted, but the overall effect was only modestly different.

Top, 1964 Continental; *bottom,* the plant at Wixom, Michigan, as it appeared in 1963.

The rear end, however, was bolder in its changes. The rear deck lid was new, allowing for another 15 percent increase in luggage capacity even over 1963's increase, and the 1961–1963 rear grille was restyled. There were two half-grilles now, one above the rear bumper and one placed in two sections in the bumper itself. They had a mesh texture similar to that of the front grille. The wheel covers were new, and reverted to the Continental emblem motif of 1961.

The biggest development of all, though, was the new 126-inch wheelbase which involved a three inch increase in the length of the rear passenger compartment. This, in turn, required the lengthening of the rear doors and the restyling of the roof, which was squared-off and increased by 5.4 inches in width. The curved side glass was dropped, too. The result was a substantial increase in interior dimensions. Head room was increased, front and rear, rear seat leg room grew by a full four inches, rear seat knee room was up by 2.5 inches and hip room was up, front and rear.

The interior was almost completely restyled, as well. The instrument panel was of an entirely new design whose main features included four built-in air conditioner outlets and a much larger glove box. New items of standard equip-

1965 Continental.

ment for 1964 included an automatic parking brake release, a trip odometer, a fuel warning light and, on the sedan, map lights and reading lights. All models had a new optional split front seat. Both sides were power operated and there was a console and padded arm rest in between.

Mechanical changes were minor. The rear end used heavier axle gears and

1965 Continental interior.

there were new "low-silhouette" 15 inch tires. The floor plan was new, necessitated by the increase in wheelbase, and had a deeper well in the trunk area that contributed to the increased capacity back there.

Total production showed a significant rise in the 1964 model year to the highest level since 1957. The same two models were available in 1964 as in recent years, and customers could choose from among eighteen new exterior colors. A total of 36,297 customers were able to make that decision. Of them, 32,969 picked the sedan and 3,328 picked the convertible.

Lincoln was making slow, but steady, inroads on the luxury market. This was all the more impressive considering that the competition was active, indeed, in this period. True, Packard was only a dim memory, but Imperial was coming on strong. For 1964, the Engel-designed model finally made its appearance, and garnered considerable attention and not a few sales. Cadillac was in the final year of the 1959 body shell, but had been heavily facelifted in 1961 and again in 1963, and would be entirely new for 1965. Through it all, the Continental steadily gained in popularity.

The 1965 Lincoln Continental was a transitional model in its styling between the 1961 design and the heavily restyled 1966 models. The 1965 models, while having very little new sheet metal, nevertheless managed to look substantially different than before.

The most noticeable alteration was the new grille which replaced the essentially vertical 1964 design. The 1965 grille was composed of horizontal bars with a slightly protruding center section and complimentary ribbed parking lights in the front fenders just above the bumper. The sheet metal on the hood and the area above the grille was new and reflected the slight center bulge of the grille.

The rear end was also revised although without any sheet metal changes. The small grille above the bumper that had first appeared in 1964 was deleted, and the two small lower grilles in the bumper itself dropped the 1964 mesh in favor of a cluster of thin horizontal ribs. The ribbed design of the parking lights was repeated on the tail lights.

The interior, new for 1964, was only moderately revised. Power front disc brakes were standard equipment, the first time they had been available. Other standard equipment included a six-way power front seat, power steering, power antenna, power door locks, automatic parking brake release, windshield washer with variable speed wipers, remote control outside mirror, map light, low fuel warning light, and front seat belts color coordinated with the interior decor.

Production increased again in 1965, rising to 40,180 units. This was the highest level since the prosperous days of the mid-1950s. A total of 36,824 sedans were produced, along with 3,356 convertibles.

By any yardstick, the 1961-series Continental was a landmark in the history of Lincoln. Following the death of the ultra-expensive, custom-built K series in 1940, the marque had spent two decades building various types of cars for various types of buyers, never seeming to find a permanent niche. In 1961, they introduced the fifth entirely new car in barely thirteen model years. Once again, the new car represented a dramatic departure from previous Lincolns, both in design and direction. This time, however, the new car formed the foundation for the unprecedented success that the marque was to enjoy during the next forty years.

CHAPTER SEVEN

Left, the one-millionth Lincoln, which was built in 1968.

Consolidation and Expansion: 1966–69

IN 1961, LINCOLN had taken a major step establishing itself as a serious challenger to Cadillac's predominance of the luxury car field with the announcement of the beautiful Lincoln Continental. In 1966, Lincoln moved to consolidate its gains and broaden the challenge by lowering prices and increasing the number of models. By the end of the decade, the reintroduction of the Mark series would expand Lincoln's presence into the lucrative personal luxury segment.

The minimum goal in 1966 was a 25 percent increase in Lincoln production. The car itself was substantially new. The basic body was the same, but everything the eye could see was redone and there were a number of important revisions underneath the skin, as well.

The 1966 Lincoln Continentals were larger cars in nearly all respects. The length was increased by five inches to 220.9, the width by an inch to 79.7 and the height by almost an inch to 55.0 (on the sedan). The wheelbase remained the same at 126 inches. Interior room remained essentially unchanged, although rear seat leg room was increased by about two inches.

The most important development by far was in the number of doors: a two-door Lincoln was offered for the first time since 1960. This model was a hardtop and was designed specifically for one-to-one competition with the highly successful Cadillac Coupe De Ville. It was given a special low price—low in comparison with recent Lincoln Continental pricing—to further its chances of success.

Indeed, all the 1966 Continentals were less expensive in a deliberate effort to cut into the De Ville market. The reduction was a little over $400 on the sedan and convertible and the two-door hardtop was almost $300 less than the sedan, so the threat was a serious one.

All of the exterior sheet metal was changed on the new models. Despite this, the now-traditional Lincoln Continental look was beautifully maintained and there could be no doubt that these were Continentals. The front treatment was very close to that of the 1965 models (which had been restyled in anticipation).

The rear treatment was, again, very similar to that of the previous year. The old textured grille sections in the back bumper were now tail lights and the back-up lights were positioned below them in the bumper. The trunk itself was increased in capacity by 2.5 cubic feet to 18, and the gas tank went from 24 gallons to 25.5.

There was other glass news in addition to the return of the curved side windows. The windshield was made of a new double-thickness vinyl laminate and convertible models had glass rear windows for the first time in several years. The convertible top could be operated from outside the car with the key-operated exterior top control option.

The interior was completely revised. The instrument panel was of a new design with all controls positioned on a pod in front of the driver, including the radio, heater, ventilation and air conditioning controls. A number of new options were offered. An automatic temperature control air conditioner was listed in addition to the conventional air conditioning unit. A stereo AM radio with tape player could be specified, as could a tilt steering wheel, transistorized ignition and a 9-inch television set that plugged into the cigarette lighter. This latter item was dealer installed and intended for use by rear passengers only.

New standard equipment included rear seat safety belts and an emergency flasher. Keys were reversible—they worked any way they were inserted—and the doors could be locked without using them. Mechanical changes included a redesigned Twin-Range Turbo-Drive transmission and an engine increased in displacement to 462 cubic inches. Horsepower also was upped to 340.

The 1966 models were well received by press and public alike, and it was obvious from the start that Lincoln-Mercury Division's hopes for the new cars were going to be fulfilled. At the beginning of the model year the division had announced to each dealer that a plan for an increase of at least 20 percent in Lincoln Continental sales would have to be submitted, working toward a national target of a minimum of 50,000 units.

It paid off. Actual production mounted to 54,755 units before the model year was over. This was a 36 percent increase over 1965 and rated as a solid success. Nearly 29 percent of the production run was composed of two-door models, while sedans accounted for 65 percent and convertibles for a shade under 6 percent.

Continental models were only mildly revised for 1967 following the exten-

Top, 1966 Continental interior; *bottom*, 1966 Continental.

sive 1966 facelift. Not much needed to be done to a car that had proven to be one of the most successful in Lincoln history, and not much was. Alterations were mostly details, but some were of interest.

Exterior changes were so minor as to be barely worth mentioning. In front, thin, vertical bars were added to the grille texture. Out back, the texture of the tail light grilles was revised. On the sides, the Continental emblem was moved from the front fender to the rear sail panel. Also, the hood ornament was spring mounted for the first time. And that, as they say, was that.

Interior modifications were only slightly more meaningful. The seat belt reminder light became standard and the deep-dish steering wheel was redesigned with a padded hub. A lane-changer feature was added to the directional signal stalk, and the optional automatic speed control was now redesigned to be stalk engaged.

An interesting option available through Lincoln dealers was a set of Continental luggage, hand stitched and custom made to fit the Continental trunk dimensions. The luggage was available in burgundy, palomino, and black.

There were several engineering changes of note. The hydraulic brake system was split in two with the front and rear brakes being separately operated.

1966 Continental.

1967 Continental.

The idea was to offer a back-up system in case one or the other system should fail. A dash warning light warned if either system experienced a pressure drop.

The automatic transmission, renamed Select-Shift Turbo-Drive, was made smoother in its operation and permitted manual shifting. The shift quadrant was also standardized to the modern PRND21. The "D" position was the fully automatic forward drive position.

A new continuous ventilation system, called Fresh-Flow, was standard. Inside air flowed into small registers located at the lower rear corner of each front door and activated one-way valves to escape to the outside. This system permitted stale, inside air to be evacuated even with the windows up.

The model line-up for 1967 was identical to that of the previous year. This was, however, the last year for the unique Lincoln Continental four-door convertible. Production never had been much with this specialized car and the final model year total was a mere 2,276, or about 5 percent of the 45,667 cars built. Total Continental production declined by 16.6 percent from the 1966 total, a development which can only be explained by the fact that both Cadillac and Imperial had essentially new cars to offer. It is also probable that an unusually large number of confirmed Lincoln customers traded to take advantage of the new models in 1966, and were therefore not in the market in 1967.

Cadillac was in the second facelift in a six-year body cycle. They had done the same with the 1959 body, facelifting it extensively in 1961 and 1963. The new 1965 body was facelifted in 1967 and would be again in 1969. For the Imperial, the 1967 model marked a rationalization of Chrysler's big car program. The Imperial had used an exclusive body shell at least since 1960, but the sales rates had never really justified it. Finally, the corporation bowed to reality and the 1967 Imperial was a gussied-up Chrysler. This did not mean Chrysler

1968 Continental.

management was through with the brand, but the days when they were willing to invest heavily in luxury cars were over.

The 1968 model year was a dramatically important one for Lincoln owing to the mid-year introduction of the Lincoln Continental Mark III. Yet, the standard 1968 Continentals were also quite different in many significant ways from previous models. Their exterior appearance was revised most significantly by the safety-related redesigning of the parking and tail lights. It was deemed necessary by the Federal Government that beginning with the 1968 model year all cars sold in the United States would have front and rear lights visible from the side. Lincoln accomplished this by building the parking lights into the front fenders and the tail lights into the rear fenders, much as they had been designed on the 1965 models. The built-in tail lights in the rear bumper now became the built-in back-up lights and the ribbed lenses more closely resembled those used in 1966 than in 1967. The front grille was also retextured and the freestanding Continental hood emblem was moved down onto the body just above the grille. The only other external alteration of note was the revised roofline on the coupe. It had a more formal appearance and rear seat passengers had a little more privacy. New "high fashion flared wheel plates" were an option.

A number of seating changes were announced, most of them in the name of safety. All 1968 coupes had self-locking seat backs, and all cars built after January 1, 1968, came fitted with front seat shoulder belts as standard equipment. Manually adjustable headrests were optional. For the bigger spenders, a new reclining passenger seat with a power adjustable headrest was offered with the optional six-way power bench seat. This same device came at no extra cost with the individually adjustable contour seat option.

Audio systems were becoming a big thing at about this time and Lincoln was anxious not to be left behind. The 1968 model saw new AM and AM/FM radio options, and the combination AM radio/stereo tape deck now included push buttons for station selection. The AM/FM signal seeking radio with power antenna also included a stereo jack to facilitate dealer installation of a stereo radio adapter.

Several engineering changes deserved mention. A redesigned "controlled crush" front end was designed to control deformation under severe crash conditions in order to better distribute the effects of the impact. The engine was slightly modified with an "Improved Combustion Emission Control System," which is to say, the first installment of the federally mandated anti-pollution gear. The Select-Shift Turbo-Drive automatic transmission was refined to offer firmer, crisper shifts. A newly designed six-terminal ignition switch accommodated dual prove-out circuits for the dual brake system light and the temperature warning light. Various weight saving measures resulted in cars that were approximately 100 pounds lighter than before, but still hovering near the 2-1/2-ton mark.

Continental sales were only middling in 1968. Standard Lincoln Continental production was hurt by the Mark III, and Mark III production did not really have a chance to get going before the end of the 1968 run. So, total 1968 model run production was only 46,904, a slight improvement over the 1967 total. Of this number, 39,134 were Lincoln Continentals and 7,770 were Lincoln Continental Mark IIIs. The 1,000,000th Lincoln—a metallic blue Continental four-door sedan—was built on Monday, March 25th.

Planning for the car that was to become the Mark III began in September, 1965. Paul F. Lorenz had been general manager of Lincoln-Mercury Division for about a year and E. F. (Gar) Laux[1] would succeed him in a little over a year later, and Laux in turn, would be succeeded by M. S. (Matt) McLaughlin six days after the Mark III's April 5, 1968, announcement. Chief stylist was L. David Ash, and he, in turn, was closely supervised by Bordinat and Lee Iacocca, then vice president in charge of American car and truck operations. Iacocca reportedly dictated the use of the classic radiator shell and the rear deck tire bulge.

The Mark III was one of the two most important cars built by Lincoln in

1968 Continental.

the postwar period—the other being the 1961 Continental. The Continental was important for having laid the foundation for Lincoln's ultimate success in the luxury field, and the Mark III was the car that built upon the foundation.

The Mark III was, perhaps more than the Mark II, built in the tradition of the original Continental. That first Continental had been a car of a rather ordinary mechanical design (based upon the medium-priced Lincoln-Zephyr) and with a price that was high, but not exorbitantly so. What made the Continental stand out, and the only reason it is so fondly remembered, was its styling. The Mark II failed because its price was arbitrarily set at a prohibitively high level and because its styling, while elegant and tasteful, was not the standout in 1956 that the original Continental's styling had been in 1940. The Mark III was a brilliant execution of the original concept. It was based upon the medium-priced Thunderbird, but modified in a sufficiently distinctive way to justify a luxury class price tag, and it was—in the opinion of many—a styling tour de force. In the opinion of many, that is, but not all, for the Mark III's styling was instantly controversial. Unlike the first Continental, the car everybody seemed to love, the Mark III was a car people either loved or hated. And there were more than a few that hated it. Eugene Bordinat was prepared for this dichotomy:

1968 Continental interior.

> We tried to be a little controversial . . . When they see it, people will be divided into two camps. Some will . . . decide they have to have it. Others wouldn't touch it with a ten foot pole . . . The buffs may not like it, but the people with money will.[2]

The people with money liked it a lot. And to be fair, quite a few buffs liked it, too, and continue to do so, but Bordinat was right about the nature of the Mark III. The hallmark of Continental styling up through the Mark II had been subtlety. The Mark III, on the other hand, was brash and proud of it. If the Continental was bought by old money, the Mark III was aimed squarely at all that new money down at the country club, new money that didn't mind showing off a little. That discovery—that people would buy good-natured ostentation—was the real importance of the Mark III. The lesson was not lost when the Mark IV was prepared for its 1972 introduction, and, eventually, even the regular Continentals would be affected. In the short run, thanks to the Mark III Lincoln sales spurred to a record level in 1969.

For years Lincolns had been achieving good reviews from the motoring press, but only mediocre sales in the marketplace. In 1969, that situation was reversed. The Mark III was not particularly well liked by the press, but the buying public loved it. Thanks largely to the post-1961 Continentals, the public was now convinced that the Lincoln was a first rate luxury car. The Mark III was the model that made the public actually want to run out and buy one. The Mark III, through most of its life, ran almost one for one with the Cadil-

1969 presidential limousine.

lac Eldorado, the first time in recent memory that a Lincoln had matched a Cadillac in head to head competition, and was further proof of the shrewdness behind the Mark III's development.

Thunderbird had gone back to body and frame construction in 1967, and so the Mark III was built that way, too. The Mark III used the stretched Thunderbird four-door chassis with the shorter two-door Thunderbird body. The result was the proper Continental proportions: a long hood—at six feet, the longest in the industry—and was unique to the Mark III, as was the interior trim. Underneath it was a different story. Most of the inner structure was borrowed or adapted from the Thunderbird. Even the instrument panel was basically a Thunderbird unit with a different outside panel. The drive-train, too, was derived from the Thunderbird.

Was the Mark III just a fancy T-Bird? Yes and No. The Mark III was a more luxurious car than its less expensive brother and built to Lincoln Continental standards, including the famous Continental 12-mile road test for each new car. Lincoln-Mercury engineers also spent a fair amount of time and money refining the Thunderbird parts they were required to share. They reduced the frame flexibility of the Mark III, and the body, too, was much stiffer. The engine, although a derivative of the Thunderbird 429, was not only good enough for a Lincoln, but supplanted the veteran Lincoln engine in other Lincoln models beginning with the 1969 model year.

The Mark III's 460 cubic inch V8 engine was hailed by Ford Motor Company as being the "most sophisticated V8 engine ever built by Ford." Although smaller than the old Continental V8 by two cubic inches, it developed 365 horsepower to the former engine's 340. The compression ratio was 10.5 to 1, an increase of two-tenths. The new engine was significantly more efficient than before, not only in terms of power and economy, but also in its burning of hydrocarbons and carbon monoxide. Since emissions control would be an increasingly important engineering problem in coming years, the new powerplant was well suited to help engineers meet the challenges immediately ahead. An improved induction system permitted a much greater flow of air to the carburetor. The intake manifold was designed to minimize air-fuel ratio variations among cylinders and permit the leanest mixtures possible. In common with other Ford engines, fuel flow was limited to optimum settings by carburetor adjustment restricters. Also included in the design was the Ford Improved Combustion (Imco) system obviating the need for a special air pump, or Thermactor, to meet current government emissions standards. The compact cylinder block was manufactured with thinwall casting, and an improved foundry technique permitted the block to be cast from eight cores, rather than the twelve used before.

The suspension was similar to the Thunderbird, with coil springs all around and a link-type stabilizer bar up front. The Mark III, however, made more extensive use of sound deadeners and rustproofing.

Except in length, the Mark III was surprisingly close to the standard Continentals in exterior dimensions. The wheelbase was nearly nine inches less at 117.2, and length was almost five inches less. The passenger compartment, however, was quite a bit smaller, and this was reflected in nearly all interior dimensions, especially in the back seat. In retrospect, and whatever else its virtues, it was an astoundingly inefficient design.

The single styling feature that stood out the most, both figuratively and literally, was the classic-style radiator shell. It was an expensive, die-cast affair that cost the company a bundle—reputedly as much as $200 a crack—but certainly earned its keep. The frontal appearance of a Mark III was wholly unlike anything else on the road, possibly excepting the Rolls-Royce. And if people jumped to the wrong conclusion, well, Lincoln-Mercury officials wouldn't mind.[3]

Headlights were hidden, but the parking lights were standard Lincoln fare. The sides, too were unadorned in the Continental style save for a subtle ridge

1969 Continental.

in the metal running lengthwise a few inches below the belt molding. The rear end sported Continental-type tail lights and the traditional Mark series Continental tire bulge in the rear deck lid. This time the bulge was purely for show—as, in a sense, was the entire car, so the bulge was a fitting design signature.

The interior was done in Sumptuous Modern décor, with everything color matched, pleated, and over-stuffed. A nylon tricot fabric was standard, although so many Marks were ordered with the optional leather that many collectors think they all came that way. The instrument panel consisted of five large, squared dial pods housing the full range of instruments. Real gauges for fuel, oil pressure, alternator and cooling system were supplemented by a wide variety of warning lights. Additional warning lights were mounted at the top of the windshield between the visors, including warnings for doors ajar, headlight doors ajar, seat belts unfastened and an unlatched trunk. A Cartier clock was listed as an option from some point late in 1968, thus beginning a long association with that design firm.

The front seat was split and individually power controlled on driver and passenger sides. Deep-cut pile carpeting was provided for floor and lower door areas, and the headlining was gabardine grain vinyl. The requisite "wood" trim was available in either fake East Indian rosewood or fake English oak.

Safety-related standard equipment on the Mark III included an energy absorbing steering wheel and column, seat belts and shoulder harnesses, and a dual braking system. Additional safety features included the Thunderbird perimeter frame and a controlled-crush front end designed to collapse in stages in the event of a frontal collision.

Other standard equipment on the Mark III included Select-Shift automatic transmission, power front disc brakes, power steering, power windows, individual power front seats, dual exhausts, flow through ventilation, center folding arm rests front and rear, a rear lamp monitoring system and a host of other typical luxury car features.

The press was less than enthusiastic. *Car Life* reported:

> Our overall impression of the Continental Mark III can best be summed up by a single word—disappointment. The car is far short on functionality, particularly in space utilization. Styling is difficult to criticize quantitatively, but the Mark III definitely is not the trendsetting, exciting, early Continental tradition.
>
> The Mark III is not, however, a bad automobile. On the contrary, the chassis and structure of the Mark III are fine examples of sound automotive engineering applied to a very luxurious vehicle. General performance is certain to be acceptable, even to critical owners. In all, the Mark III represents a polished execution of a lack-luster concept.[4]

Motor Trend reported that the Mark III "just doesn't quite turn you on."[5] Well, perhaps it didn't quite turn the staffers of *Motor Trend* "on," but, as Bordinat had predicted, it had quite the opposite effect on the luxury car buying public. Sales took off immediately and by the end of the 1969 model year were running at almost double the pace expected by Lincoln-Mercury Division. Although the Mark III did not go on sale until April of 1968, 7,770 were produced before the close of the 1968 model run. During the regular 1969 model run an additional 23,088 were manufactured for a total extended 1969 Mark III production run of 30,858. Without a doubt, the Mark III had become the most successful new model in Lincoln history. Not only was it selling at half the rate of total Lincoln production prior to its introduction, but it was on the verge of overtaking Cadillac in the personal luxury car field. Cadillac produced 24,528 Eldorados in the 1968 model year and 23,333 in 1969—a mere 245 units over the Mark III in 1969.

Although overshadowed by the hugely successful Mark III, regular Continentals were still being turned out in satisfying numbers at the Wixom plant, too. Alterations for the 1969 model year were mostly limited to refinements, since the Lincoln Continental was due for its first major overhaul since 1961 effective with the 1970 model year.

The most obvious revision in external appearance was in front where a new grille was added, influenced by the radiator style on the Mark III. It had a

1969 Continental Mark III.

mesh texture, typical of Continentals of the past, with a few strong vertical and horizontal bars, and rose in the center section to simulate a radiator. The grille and front bumper also came to a pronounced point in the center. The Continental emblem was deleted from the area above the grille in favor of the word "Continental" spelled out in block letters. It was a decidedly bolder style than that of past Continentals.

Rear end styling was revised also, but without any new sheet metal or bumper stampings. Tail lights were moved from the tops of fenders back to where they had been until 1968—in the bumper—and the grille overlay was modified to a series of thin, vertical bars. Back-up lights were moved to the fender tops, which was an unusual placement, to say the least, where they occupied the top two-thirds of the area where the tail lights had been. Reflectors were placed below them.

Interior changes were more interesting. A Town Car interior option was listed for 1969. This consisted of a special leather upholstery pattern with hidden threads, special door trim panels, color-keyed padded vinyl appliqué around the instrument cluster, wood-tone appliqué on the back of the front seat, deeper cut pile floor carpeting and a special soft nylon headliner color-keyed to the interior.

Mechanical differences for 1969, with the exception of the new 460 engine that had been phased in near the end of the 1969 model year, were too mi-

1969 Continental Mark III interior.

nor to bear reporting. The over-all length, however, was upped 3.2 inches to 224.2.

Standard and optional equipment listings were pretty much the same as before. The factory was pushing the special matched luggage again. It was a twelve-piece set of Marvelon luggage manufactured specifically for the Continental by Guild Masters.

Production of Lincoln Continentals declined by a small amount in the 1969 model run. Some of this undoubtedly was due to the success of the Mark III, and some of it was probably due to the fact that the Continental models were getting a bit long in the tooth and were due for the major change that would come the following model year. Still, production hovered near the 40,000 mark, quite good by Lincoln standards. A total of 38,290 Continentals were built, including 29,259 sedans and 9,032 coupes. When added to the Mark III production, total 1969 Lincoln production soared to a record level of 61,378 units.

In October, 1968, a new parade car was delivered to the White House. It was built as a 1968 model, but given 1969 trim before being delivered, with the actual conversion work done by Lehmann-Peterson in Chicago. The car, which was built on a special 160 inch wheelbase, was deceptively ordinary in appearance except for the design of the greenhouse. In fact, it was anything but ordinary. It was huge, almost unbelievably expensive to produce—$500,000 was rumored—and included many technological touches that had never before been used, including a number that have never been revealed. The vehicle was over twenty-one feet in length.

The car included the same type of concealed platform in back that the two 1968 follow-up cars had pioneered, together with the deck-mounted retractable grip handles. Two tons of armor were reportedly built into the body. Rubber-edge steel discs inside the tires were designed to permit speeds as high as 50 mph even with all four tires shot out. The roof line was raised two inches over that of the standard Continental sedan, and featured a special type of clear glass paneling over the rear compartment. The glass, developed by PPG Industries, was bulletproof.

The exterior was finished in black, and a detachable black vinyl cover could be used over the entire roof for more formal, or less public, occasions. In a parade situation, a center section of the roof could be raised on hinges to permit the occupants to stand. The interior was finished in silver-gray upholstery and mouton carpeting. The fabrics were the same as those used in the Continental Mark III. An exceptionally powerful air conditioning system with twelve outlets (six on either side) was fitted to help fight the "greenhouse effect" of the greenhouse. A public address system was available, as well as a sound system designed to transmit outside noises into the rear compartment so that cheering multitudes should be heard as well as seen. Finally, six tiny spot lights built into the tops of the front fenders offered just the right amount of illumination at night for the bumper-mounted U.S. and presidential flags.

In sum, the decade had been a dramatic and exciting one for Lincoln. All the false starts and missteps of the early postwar period were forgotten in the golden glow of success. Lincoln at last had its mission. All that seemed left now was to keep up the heat and wait for Cadillac to falter.

CHAPTER EIGHT

President Ford campaigns in the 1972 presidential limousine.

Let the Good Times Roll: 1970–76

THE GOOD TIMES were finally rolling for Lincoln as the new decade dawned. The Continental sedan had established itself as a competitive force in the mainstream luxury market against Cadillac's sedan range, while the new Mark III had been a smash hit from the very beginning in the personal luxury segment. After a quarter-of-a-century of mostly failures, Lincoln had its mission down pat. When Bennett E. Bidwell was named general manager in March, the only challenge on his desk seemed to be doing more of the same.

The Lincoln Continental was the big news in 1970. It had its first all-new body since 1961, and was designed under the direction of Eugene Bordinat to steal buyers from other luxury marques—i.e., Cadillac. While the new Continental styling was in most ways simply an extension of 1961–69 themes, the new models were different in many important ways from the models of the previous year.

The most significant single change was the abandonment of unibody construction in favor of traditional body-and-frame. The Mark III had used body-and-frame from the beginning and now, with the conversion of the Continental, the entire Wixom plant was switched over. The new Continentals, following the lead of the Mark III, were designed to use other Ford automotive components, notably those of the large Mercurys and Fords. By this time, the Mercurys were practically as large and it simply didn't make sense not to take advantage of production economies where they were feasible.

The new car was almost 300 pounds lighter than before, yet was virtually the exact same physical size. Overall length and height were increased by mere fractions of an inch, while width was actually less. Wheelbase was up an inch, and tread was substantially wider by 1.9 inches in front and 3.3 inches in the rear. The interior was much roomier in most important dimensions. Luggage capacity, too, was increased—to 19 cubic feet. The 1970 Continental was, in short, a far more efficient design than the one it replaced.

The styling was definitely Continental with perhaps something of a GM flavor to it. This was deliberate, as Lincoln designers were intentionally seeking to win favor with the confirmed GM—and particularly Cadillac—buyers. It was for this reason that the traditional Continental clam-shell, center-opening doors on sedans were deleted in favor of more normal front-hinged rear doors. A survey was taken in which it was learned that while Lincoln owners liked the clam-shells, Cadillac owners did not, and so the doors were changed.

The die-cast grille was reminiscent of the 1966 Continental, but with concealed headlights. The front end was much more aggressively sculptured than on past Continentals. Cornering lights were located on the sides in the wraparound front bumpers. These operated when the directional signal switch was used (assuming the headlights were on). Running lights were also a part of this same unit. They worked with the parking/directional lamps, and similar units were placed in the wraparound rear bumper. Sides were basically unadorned, and the rear end, too, was pretty much traditional Continental fare. The massive tail light/back-up light assemblies were built into the rear bumper. The windshield wipers were concealed under a hood extension, the side vent windows were done away with, and the rear wheels were concealed by fender skirts. Continental script appeared on the rear quarter panels and the left headlight cover. Continental emblems were placed on the deck lid, the sail panels, and in front above the grille.

The interior was likewise completely restyled. Doors were wider for easier entry and exit. Front doors on sedans were six inches wider, and the back doors were four inches wider. Doors on coupe models were a full seven inches wider. The new seats were deeper, front to back, and the rear seat was raised four inches to allow for a more comfortable seating position in the rear compartment. Center arm rests were fitted, front and rear, and the door had padded rests that also contained power window, power seat, and remote control mirror controls. The Town Car trim option first offered in 1969 was returned for 1970.

The instrument panel was also of a new design, and the steering wheel was a three spoke, "modified oval" type that offered more seat clearance and a better view of the instruments. A number of safety-related features were offered, including three-point lap and shoulder belts, a locking steering column, and a new tamper-resistant odometer. For two-door models, an automatic seat back release was optional. A new flow-through ventilation system, similar to that on the Mark III was also standard. All models were available in a wide

Top, 1970 Continental interior; *bottom*, 1970 Continental.

range of exterior finishes, including four new metal-flake colors, called "Stardust," an imitation of Cadillac's popular Firemist colors.

Although the Continental body was entirely new, the drive-train was not. The same 460 V8 returned with a couple of minor modifications such as an improved water pump and better accessory drive belting. Coil-link suspension, similar to that used on the Mark III, was employed, and fiberglass belted tires were standard. An important option was the new Sure-Track Brake System. This computer-controlled system developed by Kelsey-Hayes markedly improved braking stability by preventing rear wheel lock-up, even on ice or snow.

Press reaction to the new Lincoln Continental was highly favorable. *Motor Trend*, which hadn't thought much of the Mark III, said of the new Continental: "If it's possible to improve an already excellent luxury car, we think Lincoln has."[1]

As for the Mark III, it was the recipient of a number of detail improvements for the 1970 model year. On the outside there were new wheel covers. The parking and tail lights were subjected to revisions of the most minor sort, and the windshield wipers were concealed, as on the big Lincolns. The vinyl roof was standard equipment for the first time—has anyone ever seen a 1969 Mark III without one?—and a power-operated sun roof was listed as an option.

1970 Continental.

The Mark III interior was similarly refined. Upholstery patterns were slightly revised, and power seat controls were moved to the door arm rests along with the window and remote mirror controls. The 1970 interior featured real walnut veneer on the instrument panel, steering wheel and doors. The steering wheel was of the Continental modified oval design. A new standard feature was the right-hand visor vanity mirror. Another was a time-delay map light device which was activated when the driver's door was opened and provided eight to ten seconds of passenger compartment illumination before automatically shutting off. The Mark III shared other interior features with the Continental, including the three-point seat belt/shoulder harness, tamper resistant odometer and locking steering column. The Continental automatic seat back latch was standard. One final touch: a Cartier clock was now standard equipment.

Mechanical changes were few. The Sure-Track Brake System, optional on the Continental, was standard on the Mark III. Michelin 225-15 steel belted radial tires were standard equipment, and came with a 40,000 mile wear guarantee.

The famous Lincoln Continental 12-mile road test was retained for all Lincoln models. It was, however, moved indoors where it was scientifically simu-

1970 Continental Mark III.

lated. Sales gains in the previous few years had made the real thing harder and harder to maintain.

Still, Lincoln sales were off slightly in 1970. This was due primarily to the state of the economy, but the production total—59,127 for the model year—was the second best in Lincoln history. This consisted of 37,695 Continentals and 21,432 Mark IIIs.

Lincoln Continental and Mark III models were little changed for Lincoln's Golden Anniversary year in 1971. The Continental models were the most visibly altered, particularly in the front end. The grille was revised once again, as in 1969, to present an appearance more in keeping with the classic radiator theme of the Mark III without departing too much from traditional Continental practice. The 1971 grille ran only the width of the center bulge. The headlights remained covered, as before. The rear end was slightly revised.

The most important change to the interior was the revision of upholstery patterns. Automatic temperature control air conditioning was made standard along with tinted glass. Michelin radials were listed as an option and an automatic sun roof could be purchased by special order through Lincoln dealers. The special "Stardust" metallic colors of 1970 were supplanted by "Moondust" colors in four shades.

The Town Car option was not in the catalogue at the beginning of the 1971

1971 Continental.

model year, but it was revived in mid-year as the "Golden Anniversary Continental." Trim was essentially the same as before with several added touches. The car was identified as a Town Car by block letters on the lower part of the front fenders. Other amenities included a limited-edition plaque on the instrument panel, the owner's initials on black and gold on the front doors, and a boxed set of 22 karat gold finished ignition and door keys.

Engineering modifications were minor. The 460 V8 had a new fuel evaporative emissions control system, front and rear tread was increased by two inches to 64.3 inches, and steel guard rails were built into the doors to provide added protection against side collisions.

Changes to the Mark III were even less cosmic. Automatic temperature control air conditioning and tinted glass were made standard equipment. Front seats were of a new high back design featuring built-in head rests, but the upholstery pattern remained the same. The sun roof became a regular factory option.

Sales rebounded sharply in 1971. Production which had been running at a one-to-four ratio with Cadillac in 1970, rose to a one-to-three ratio. Total Lincoln production for the model run was 62,642. This included 35,551 Continentals and 27,091 Mark IIIs.

The Mark III was once more running neck and neck with the Eldorado,

1971 Continental Mark III.

1971 Continental Town Car interior.

with fewer than 300 units separating them for the 1971 model year. This was especially significant because the Eldorado was entirely new, while the Mark III was at the end of its product life cycle. As a confirmation that Lincoln stylists had a better sense of what luxury car buyers wanted than did their counterparts at Cadillac, this fact would be hard to beat. Also a mystery is why Chrysler never tried in this era to field a luxury personal car with its faltering Imperial brand. In fact, it had no large personal-type cars to compete against anything Ford or GM offered, such as the Thunderbird or the Pontiac Grand Prix. Eventually, such models would appear but, in the case of the Imperial, it was both far too little and far too late.

The 1972 model year marked yet another major advance in Lincoln's coming of age as a luxury contender. Sales and production reached unprecedented levels with the introduction of a new Mark. Styled by Wes Dahlberg, the Mark IV represented the ultimate flowering of the marketing strategy behind the Mark III. Everything the Mark III had done so well, the Mark IV did even better. Where the styling of the Mark III had seemed to many observers to be a bit choppy, the Mark IV was smooth and sleek and almost perfectly proportioned.

The Mark IV was four inches longer and half-an-inch lower than the Mark III. The wheelbase, too, was stretched to 120.4 inches. Head room and rear seat hip room suffered somewhat in the new model, but most interior dimensions were up. It was an impressive package despite the fact that it shared an increasing number of parts with the less expensive Thunderbird. The exterior sheet metal, except for the roof, was unique to the Mark, but the interior was becoming noticeably less different. The instrument panels were so much alike that Mark IVs started showing up on dealer lots with Thunderbird script on them, and vice versa. The Thunderbird buyers seemed not to mind.

Feature for feature the Mark III and the Mark IV were so close that the Mark IV's real distinction clearly lay in its styling. The proportions were even more "Continental" than before. The hood was longer, the rear deck was shorter, and the resulting vehicle more closely resembled a show car than a production car. Special exterior features included a stand-up hood ornament, recessed door handles and an unusual opera window with an etched silver leaf Continental star.

The opera window was standard but it could be deleted on special order in favor of the traditional Mark bright star ornament. It is unrecorded how many, if any, were built without the window, though. The new version of the classic radiator-style Mark grille was bolder than before, and dipped down into the front bumper. This left it dangerously exposed to front end collisions, so an optional bumper guard was available.

The interior, as has been noted, was completely redone in similar fashion with the Thunderbird. The Mark was different in the details of its upholstery patterns, and the front of the instrument panel was somewhat restyled. The general quality of the materials used on the Mark IV was superior, as one would expect, but the quality of assembly cannot have been much different despite Lincoln-Mercury's claims at the time.

A regular fuel version of the 460 V8 was standard on the Mark IV. Important mechanical changes were limited to those mandated by the government. The front suspension was essentially a carry-over, but the rear suspension was a new four-link design with deep-coil springs, double-acting hydraulic shock absorbers, and a stabilizer bar.

The Lincoln Continental sedan and coupe were subjected to minor modifications, most of them on the exterior. The grille was revised into a mesh pattern rather similar to the 1969 grille, and the little ornamental grilles on the headlight covers were similarly revised. Except for the most minor changes to the instrument panel, there were hardly any changes at all to the interior.

The mid-1971 Town Car option was continued over for 1972 in essentially unchanged form, minus the special instrument panel plaque and gold keys. In late-January a new Town Car was announced. This car, specified as a 1972-1/2 model, was different in many details from the earlier version. The standard

Top, 1972 factory scene; *bottom*, pinstriping a Continental Mark IV.

leather upholstery was dropped, although still available as an option, in favor of beige or black Lamont cloth. The rear compartment came with assist straps and individual reading lamps. The luggage compartment, including the spare tire, was carpeted. A unique feature of the Town Car was the new "mini vent" windows. These were featured in each front door, and had the appearance of small vent windows. They did not, however, open in the normal fashion, but retracted along with the power windows, in sequence, first the mini vents, then the side windows. In addition, each Town Car owner received a set of silver-plated keys and a set of monograms for mounting on the front doors.

A total of 94,560 Lincolns were built during the 1972 model run. This was 50 percent greater than any previous Lincoln record. Mark IV production was up an astonishing 79 percent to 48,591 units and Continental production was up by 29 percent to 45,969. In the upper luxury market supplied by Lincoln, Cadillac, and Imperial, Lincoln accounted for 25.8 percent of total sales during the calendar year. This was the highest penetration in Lincoln history. Total industry penetration was 0.9 percent which, again, was a Lincoln record, beating the previous high (in 1956) by 25 percent. Moreover, Lincoln was now selling at a better than one to three ratio to Cadillac, up from one to four in the late 1960s and one to five in the early 1960s. Best of all, the brand, which had reputedly lost as much as $60,000,000 during 1958–60, had now become a solid financial asset to the corporation.

Even the president got a new Lincoln. In 1970, another presidential parade

1972 Continental Town Car.

1972 Continental Mark IV.

car was commissioned by the Secret Service so that the 1961 edition could be retired. This new car, delivered in 1972, closely followed the 1969 limousine in most important details. The exterior was black, while the rear compartment was upholstered in medium-gray leather in essentially the same pattern as the 1972 Town Sedan.

The following model year, 1973, was one of consolidation with the production cars. After a slow start, the 1970 Continental design was finally achieving wide popular acceptance. The Mark IV, new in 1972, had been instantaneously successful beyond Lincoln-Mercury Division's wildest hopes, and became even more so in 1973. This was the year Lincoln finally cracked the century mark in production. Well over 100,000 units were built before the close of the model run.

All 1973 Lincolns sported the new federally mandated five miles per hour front bumpers and two-and-a-half miles per hour rear bumpers. These were intended to provide added protection in low speed collisions, particularly to items such as lights that were essential to safe vehicle operation. They were also responsible for most of the approximately one hundred pounds of additional weight in the new models. The 460 V8 engine common to all Lincoln models was subjected to the latest emission standards with resultant operational problems and loss of fuel efficiency. It is largely for this reason that the 1973 models are widely regarded as being the least desirable from this period—and it was true of other American cars, too. A couple of theft deterrent features were standard on the new models, including an inside hood latch release and a spare tire lock.

The 1973 Lincoln Continental was almost untouched from the previous year. Just about the only way to tell a 1973 from the outside is the Continental name spelled out in block letters across the front of the car, just above the grille. And, of course, by the presence of the 5 mph bumper, which jutted out visibly more than before. Interior alterations were limited to a different standard brocade upholstery fabric (which nevertheless looked pretty much like the old one). Other options for 1973 included a new AM/FM multiplex radio with a stereo type system, a right-hand remote control rear-view mirror, and new all electric door locks.

A new Town Coupe was added to the successful Town Car (sedan) option. The standard upholstery fabric for 1973 was Victoria velour, marking the early stages of the velour fad of the 1970s. The Town Car/Coupe nameplate was moved to the sail panel and the mini vents were not standard. Other than that, there were few changes from 1972.

The Mark IV was even less changed than the Continental. The differences in standard equipment have already been noted. It could, however, boast a few interesting new options, some of them at announcement time and some in mid-year. One option not mentioned was the 1972 opera window delete option. They all came with opera windows now.

The first of the series of special décor options for which Lincoln was to become noted as the decade progressed appeared on the 1973 Mark IV. This was the Silver Luxury Group Option, and consisted of silver exterior finish with a special silver vinyl top and cranberry red Victoria velour inside. Other new options mentioned for the Continental also applied to the Mark IV.

In March, a special silver "moonroof" Mark IV went on sale. This model featured a special glass panel designed to compliment the car's exterior. The glass was tinted and a manually operated sliding sunshade could be closed from the inside to block out all outside light. The exterior was silver with a silver vinyl top and the interior was silver leather.

An anti-theft alarm system was also announced in March. By this time the Mark IV was sufficiently popular with certain elements of society that it was estimated that as many as one-third of all Mark IVs on the road in urban areas were stolen. This system included an electric alarm that activated the horn whenever a door or the rear deck lid was opened. The system was armed with the door lock (ignition) key, and disarmed by unlocking either front door with the same key. In May, solid state ignition was announced as an option on the Mark IV, replacing conventional ignition parts such as points, cam and condenser with reliable, low maintenance solid state electronic components.

A couple of tidbits from 1973: William P. Benton replaced Bennett E. Bidwell as general manager of Lincoln-Mercury Division in March. Then, in

June, during his state visit to the United States, a Town Car was presented to Soviet Party Secretary Brezhnev by President Nixon. The car was finished in dark blue with a black vinyl top and a black velour interior. The gift included a supply of spare parts and an engraved plaque noting the occasions.

Production in 1973 soared to the almost unbelievable record of 128,073 units. This included 58,636 Continentals and 69,437 Mark IVs for the model year. By the end of the 1973 calendar year, Mark IV production was running an astonishing 38 percent ahead of Cadillac's Eldorado. Lincoln was fast approaching the sort of predominance in the luxury personal car market that Cadillac had so long enjoyed in the general luxury car market.

The following year was another one in which Lincoln's position in the luxury field was consolidated and reinforced by means of numerous modifications and refinements in the existing product line. The government, of course, had its special input into the 1974 models. The new Lincolns had redesigned front and rear bumpers for the second year in a row in order to meet federal collision standards. This was also the year of the notorious seat belt interlock system, another government goodie that required the driver and passenger to buckle themselves in advance of engaging the ignition or the car would not operate. In the event this schedule was not met within a measured period of time, the entire sequence, for both driver and passenger, would have to com-

1973 Continental Mark IV.

mence from scratch. This device holds the singular distinction of being the only federally mandated safety or economy standard ever to become sufficiently unpopular with the general public that it had to be repealed by Congress. But not, alas, before the conclusion of the 1974 model run.

Another Lincoln standard feature for 1974 was solid state ignition in all models, and the Hydro-boost braking system was put into production toward the tail end of the model run. This system fed the power brakes with hydraulic—rather than vacuum—power and had a reservoir device that would permit powered braking even with the engine off. Other news was that the windshield washers were now mounted on the wiper arms. All Lincoln models featured some new accessories, including an illuminated visor vanity mirror, the moonroof that made its appearance on the 1973-1/2 Mark IV, and a "headlight convenience group" that combined automatic operating and time-delay functions.

The Continental was the most changed of the two Lincoln lines, at least in appearance. The front and rear ends were restyled. The front was simplified from the 1973 design.

The Continental interior was only slightly modified. Coupe models had the automatic seat back release as part of their standard equipment for the first time, and all models came with the six-way power seat and the Cartier

1973 Continental Mark IV interior.

clock. New Continental options included the Mark IV's anti-theft alarm system and, for the standard models, a fully carpeted luggage compartment.

The Mark IV was virtually unchanged in appearance except for the new federal bumpers and the wrap-around tail lights that were of a similar design to those on the Continental. Power mini vent windows were optional, as was a new "quick defrost" system that was supposed to be three-to-five times more efficient than the old system. It used tiny electrical wires imbedded in the front and rear windshields.

The really big news with the Mark IV was the expanding list of special luxury décor options. The Silver Luxury Group Option returned, but this year it was available with a choice of silver or red leather or cranberry Media velour trim. The silver tinted moonroof was optional. A Gold Luxury Group Option was new for 1974. It featured unique gold Diamond Fire paint with a gold flare levant grain vinyl roof. The interior was mostly tan leather with dark brown accent stripes. In February a Saddle and White trim package was announced. This car was white with a saddle vinyl roof and white leather seats with saddle accent stripes.

Production lagged in 1974 due to the Arab oil embargo and the resultant recession. It would be two years before industry sales fully recovered, but Lincoln production was down only 26 percent and still rated as the third best

1974 Continental.

year in the marque's history. A total of 93,985 Lincolns were built during the model run. Of these, 57,316 were Mark IVs and 36,669 were Continentals. By any standard other than that of 1973, it was a terrific year.

In 1975, the auto industry began to recover a bit from the doldrums of 1974, and Lincoln sales were fueled by the popularity of the restyled Continental. The Mark IV, on the other hand, declined somewhat in popularity, but not enough to keep 1975 from being the second best year in Lincoln history. There was also a notable change in the front office this year. William P. Benton, who had replaced Bennett E. Bidwell as general manager of Lincoln-Mercury Division in March, 1973, was himself replaced by Walter S. Walla in July, 1975.

The Continental was rather cleverly restyled. It looked like an entirely new car. In fact, only about half of the sheet metal was really different. The interior was retrimmed, but other than that it was the same Continental dealers had been selling for five years.

The most obvious new feature was the roofline. It was much more square than on previous Continentals and front and rear side windows were separated on sedans with a wide center pillar similar to that being used on the Cadillac Fleetwood since 1971. Vinyl roofs were standard and both the sedan and the coupe had rear opera windows with Continental stars laminated into the glass. The opera window on the sedan was an oval type, while the coupe

1974 Continental Mark IV.

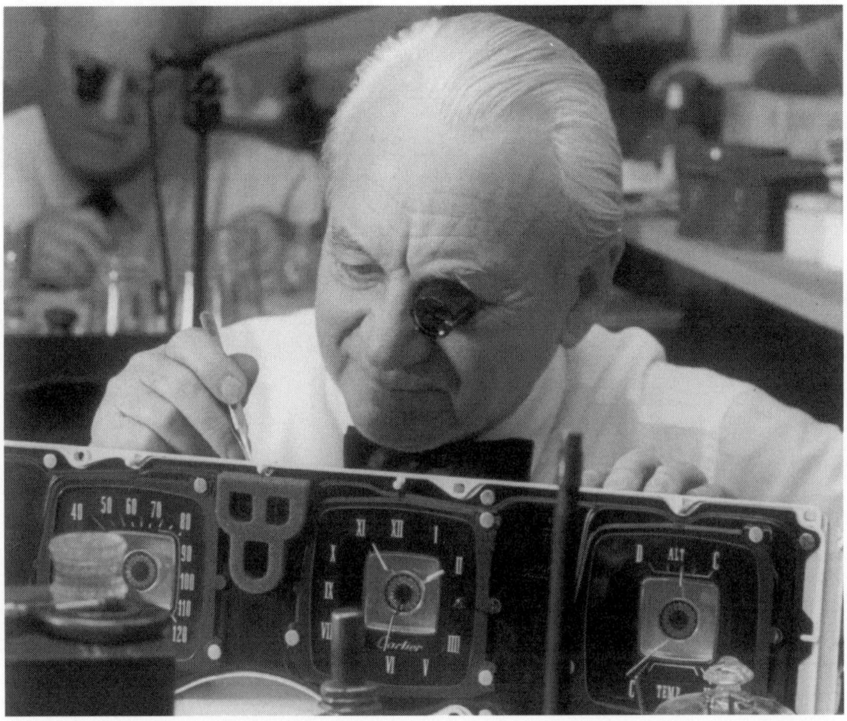

Installing a Cartier clock in 1975.

window was more normal in its configuration. In addition, Town Car models had a standard outside coachlamp built into the center pillar. This lamp could be ordered as an option on base Continentals. A three-quarter vinyl roof option was listed in mid-year at $104 for the Town Coupe and at $164 for the coupe. Due to the new roofline, the 1975 Continentals, and especially the coupes, were noticeably roomier than before.

The Continental interior was substantially restyled. The instrumental panel was redone, the steering wheel was of a new design, and upholstery and trim patterns and fabrics were revised. Town Car models had a glove box vanity mirror as standard and new "loose pillow" style seats in leather or Media velour.

A new AM/FM Multiplex stereo radio was made standard in February. Four-wheel disc brakes were listed as an option. An extended range fuel tank was also listed in the accessory catalogue. This was an auxiliary tank of approximately eight gallons capacity that filled up through the regular filler pipe by means of an over-flow.

In April, a specially priced Continental coupe was announced for production commencing on April 28th. This car was offered in response to dealer requests and was a regular Coupe with several items of standard equipment deleted, including door edge guards, license plate frames, vinyl side moldings, upper body paint stripes, remote deck lid release, power door locks, AM/FM Multiplex radio, and floor mats. The car was retailed at $8,799, plus any Lincoln options except the Town Car option.

Visual changes to the Mark IV were of the most minor variety. The front bumper guards were slightly modified and the standard full-vinyl side windows and windshield. Four-wheel disc brakes, the new style tilting steering wheel, automatic speed control, front and rear carpeting floor mats, remote control

Top, 1975 Continental interior; *bottom*, 1975 Continental.

rear deck lid and, after February, the AM/FM Multiplex stereo radio were among the new standard features. New items of optional equipment included forged aluminum wheels, filigreed vinyl side moldings, wide band whitewall tires, and a power lumbar seat. This latter option was designed to provide variable support for the driver's lower back and was adjustable through a range of 1.7 inches by means of a seat-mounted switch.

The popular Silver Luxury Group Option returned for 1975. A landau vinyl roof was optional. The Saddle and White Luxury Group also returned with a revised interior. The seats were cream with dark brown trim for 1975. A new option was the Lipstick and White Luxury Group featuring a solid white exterior (with optional landau vinyl roof) and white seats and doors with lipstick red trim. The final new option was the Blue Diamond Luxury Group. This option came with aqua blue Diamond Fire paint and aqua blue crushed Media velour upholstery.

All 1975 Lincolns were fitted with the new federally-mandated catalytic converters as part of the updated emissions system. The converters required the use of unleaded gasoline.

Lincoln sales rebounded in 1975 and model year production rose to 101,843. This included 47,145 Mark IVs and 54,698 Continentals. It was a two-brand race now. A quarter-of-a-century of on again–off again effort had failed to es-

1975 Continental Mark IV.

tablish the Imperial in the luxury field, and Chrysler bowed to the inevitable and discontinued it.

Lincoln models offered virtually nothing new of any functional consequence in 1976 other than modifications required by the government in order to meet the latest fuel economy and emissions standards. Styling, too, was untouched, both inside and out. All of the important developments were with regard to optional equipment. A number of new luxury décor options were available on the Mark IV, and, in an effort to keep base prices down, both the Continental and Mark IV began charging for a number of things that had formerly been standard. The base price of the Coupe was reduced by $72, the Sedan by $363.

The number of optional décor groups offered with the Mark IV became bewildering. There were eight luxury groups for 1976, and six of them were of a new "mix and match" type that allowed for a certain number of variations within each group. In addition, there were four entirely new Designer Series Mark IVs, each "designed" by a famous designer from a non-automotive field.

The eight luxury décor groups for 1976 were the Blue Diamond, Saddle/White and Lipstick White groups of 1975, plus the "refreshingly new" Red/Rosé, Jade/White, Dark Jade/Light Jade, Gold/Cream and Versailles groups. All except the Versailles and Blue Diamond groups came with two-tone

1976 Continental.

leather and vinyl interiors, and any combination of vinyl top, paint, paint striping and body side molding in one or both of the special two colors chosen for each individual group. In other words, the Gold/Cream Group came with a gold and cream interior according to the factory's design, but the exterior could be had in any combination of gold or cream—or all gold or all cream if the buyer desired it that way.

Top, 1976 Continental Mark IV interior; *bottom*, 1976 Continental Mark IV.

Some items, such as the landau half-roof, the body moldings and the paint striping were extra cost even over the cost of the luxury décor group, but it could only be ordered in the approved shades that went with that particular group. The Versailles Option (remember that name because it pops up in the Lincoln story!) by contrast to the other groups involved no contrast at all. It was a monotone group featuring crushed velour upholstery and came in four shades: medium blue, jade, tan and red. If the red group was ordered, for example, the entire car, even including the trim in the luggage compartment, was red.

The four Designer Series Marks were named after Cartier, Givenchy, Bill Blass, and Emilio Pucci. These designers or their representatives participated in the color and trim coordination of the cars named for them. All four had the designer's signature in the opera window and on a 22-carat gold plate on the instrument panel. The plate also carried the purchaser's name.

The Cartier edition was a monochromatic grey with velour upholstery and red pinstriping. The Givenchy edition was turquoise with white top and side moldings, black and white pinstripes and turquoise velour upholstery. The Bill Blass edition was dark blue with cream top and side moldings, cream and gold pinstripes and either navy velour upholstery or dark blue and cream leather and vinyl upholstery. The Emilio Pucci edition was burgundy with silver top and side molding, silver and red pinstripes and burgundy velour upholstery.

There were several new items of optional equipment that were available on both Continental and Mark IV models. The AM/FM Multiplex stereo radio was available with an automatic station scanning function or with a Quadrasonic 8-track tape deck. An engine block heater was also listed, and the tinted one-way moonroofs were offered in silver, gold, brown, light jade or rosé.

Lincoln production reached near record levels in 1976. A total of 124,756 cars were built, including 56,110 Mark IVs and 68,646 Continentals.

Despite a down year or two, the 1970s had been heady, indeed, for the people at Lincoln-Mercury. Cadillac had put up a stiff fight across the boards, but Lincoln had made solid inroads. Meanwhile, Imperial had been vanquished entirely. It appeared that good times would roll on and on forever. It had been almost too easy. Someone should have recalled the old saying that when things seem too good to be true they probably are . . .

CHAPTER NINE

The 1977 Versailles press preview.

Storm Clouds Gather: 1977–84

SALES CONTINUED to register satisfying gains throughout the mid-1970s when taken as a percentage of the industry total. The industry, unfortunately, was suffering, first because of the Arab Oil Embargo of late 1973 and because of the ensuing recession during 1974 and 1975. Within Ford Motor Company, there had been heated debate over the future of the big Lincolns.

Henry Ford II and Lee Iacocca reportedly wound up on the opposite sides of the issue, each with active partisans on his side. The Ford faction wished to downsize the big Fords and Mercurys in 1979 and the big Lincolns in 1980, with the sub-compact Escort/Lynx project delayed until 1981. Iacocca, so the story goes, pushed for just the reverse: the Escort/Lynx car in 1979 and the big cars in 1981. It was a question of priorities and of how marketing trends were perceived.

Unfortunately, when the downsized Fords, Mercurys and Lincolns were announced, the market had made a 180 degree shift. Big cars were suddenly all but unsalable in a market that was screaming for small cars. In that, Cadillac and Lincoln reacted very differently to the crisis. Cadillac rushed a compact luxury car, the Seville, through to a mid-1975 introduction and set to work with other GM divisions on an elaborate project to downsize all GM big cars for the 1977 model year.

Ford Motor Company preferred, for the short-term, to concentrate its efforts on the lower end of the price spectrum. The initial program resulted in the Zephyr and Fairmont cars announced for the 1978 model year. The Continental had been given a facelift for the 1975 run. The popular Mark series was scheduled for a complete reskinning in 1977 and a Seville-type compact was also in the works for mid-year announcement. Lincoln's more conservative approach resulted in part from the parent corporation's decision to concentrate resources elsewhere and partly from uncertainty as to the ultimate success of the sort of downsizing contemplated by Cadillac. Accordingly, when the 1977 Cadillacs were finally announced, Lincoln officials were no less interested at the reception than their counterparts at Cadillac. It proved highly favorable in most respects, after a certain initial amount of culture shock.

If the downsized Cadillacs were doing well, the 1977 Mark and Continental were ravenously received by the car buying public. Sales and production soared to previously unheard-of levels. Mark production—80,321 units—was

1977 Continental.

close to double the Eldorado total. Continental production—95,600 units—was the best ever and better than total Lincoln production for any year up to 1973. It was a moment of great pride for Lincoln management, but not one of unalloyed joy, for there were storm clouds on the not-too-distant horizon.

It seemed that just as Lincoln had mastered the rules of the game the rules had begun to change. The Arab Oil Embargo had not only increased the cost of petroleum, it had, for the first time, cast doubts on the security of the West's sources of supply. Conservation suddenly became an urgent national goal, and when that happened cars like the Continental and the Mark were instantly transformed from state-of-the-art luxury vehicles into dinosaurs whose demise was inevitable.

The year began with business as usual but soon hit a serious snag. A UAW strike complicated the fall new model announcement, but failed to cause any lasting damage. Also, there was an important personnel change at the top: Walter S. Walla was succeeded in October, 1977, by Walter J. Oben.

Both the Continental and the Mark offered a stunning array of lavish interior options. Lincoln interiors had been getting more elaborate and varied as the decade progressed, but now they reached for unbelievable levels. Even the exalted Cadillac Fleetwood sedan was beginning to look a trifle plain by comparison, and Cadillac designers were forced to put in overtime to keep up. As if all that weren't enough, the compact Versailles was officially announced on March 28th. Together with a revitalized national economy, these efforts resulted in the all-time best year of production in Lincoln's history.

The new Continental and Mark V models all featured reduced maintenance schedules and a new standard AM/FM monaural radio, replacing the old AM unit. A number of interesting options were listed for the first time. These included an illuminated entry system (the interior lights went on when the front doors were opened), a CB radio, turbine style cast aluminum wheels, an electrically heated left-hand remote control mirror, and an electrically retractable moonroof.

The Continental was the recipient of a Mark-style stand-up radiator grille for 1977. This sort of frontal design was pretty much a Lincoln trademark by now, so it made a lot of sense to extend it to the Continental, too. Practically nothing else on the car was altered, however. The 1977 model looked different, but, except for the grille, it really wasn't. The 460 V8 was still standard, but a 400 cubic inch two-barrel powerplant was used in California.

Two interesting new options exclusive to the Continental were a wide fixed glass moonroof, much larger than before, and a Williamsburg Town Car option. The Continental had been growing a bit gaudy for some peoples' liking, and this model was Lincoln's response. It was simplicity itself. The wide body side moldings, the opera windows and the coach lamps were all deleted. Two color schemes were offered: silver/grey and dark/midnight cordovan.

The Mark V was entirely new on the outside and heavily revised on the inside for 1977. The dimensions throughout were almost identical to those of the 1976 Mark IV. The principal differences were in the trunk space (21 percent more) and in the overall weight (nearly 500 pounds less). It was still a

1977 Continental Mark V.

big, big car, though. The new body styling was much more angular than it had been on the Mark IV. All the familiar Mark series touches were in evidence and a new one: three functional louvers in the front fender just behind the front wheel. The Mark was even less subtle than before, but, then, it had never been intended for subtle people.

The usual bewildering array of interior décor options was listed in the catalogue. The Luxury Groups were down to five: Gold/Cream, Cordovan, Midnight Blue/Cream, Red/Rosé, and Light Jade/Dark Jade. The four Designer Edition models returned in name, although the colors were different.

Mechanically, the Mark V was little changed. The major departure was the standard 400 cubic inch two-barrel V8. The old 460 V8 was optional, except in California.

Lincoln-Mercury made its first attempt to confront downsizing in 1977—although not by choice. For a number of years, several foreign makes—most notably Mercedes-Benz—had been proving that Americans would pay real money for compact luxury cars. This fact had been ignored as long as humanly possible, but the suddenly emergent energy crisis forced Cadillac and Lincoln to come to terms with reality (Chrysler had dropped out of the luxury field when it discontinued the Imperial in 1975). Cadillac rushed its Seville to completion in the spring of 1975. Its reception was enthusiastic and Lincoln had no choice but to follow suit.

Lincoln was operating under the shadow of another threat, too: the 1975 corporate fuel economy standards (CAFE) imposed upon the various companies by the U.S. Government. Each year the average fuel economy level of all the vehicles produced by each auto maker was due to increase—to 19 mpg in 1979, to 20 mpg in 1980 and to 27.5 mpg by 1985. That meant that for every Lincoln sold, a couple of Ford Pintos or Mercury Bobcats would have to be sold to compensate. If that were the extent of the problem, Lincoln could presumably have gone on indefinitely, so long as Ford Motor Company's small car sales held up. Unfortunately, there was a lower limit set to rise each year, and any car failing to meet that minimum mpg standard would be subjected to a "gas guzzler" tax of increasing severity.

So, like it or not, Lincolns were going to have to be downsized; like it or not, Lincoln was going to have to learn how to build competitive smaller cars. The only question was when. The Lincoln response to the Seville challenge was urgently required, if only to prove to the public that Lincoln could build smaller cars just as well as Cadillac if it really wanted to. The downsizing of the big Lincoln and the Mark was a different matter. The big Lincolns would wait.

The compact Lincoln Versailles was announced to the public on March 28,

1977. By a stroke of coincidence, it was built in the old Wayne plant in which all Lincolns had been built between 1952 and 1957. The reception was a distinctly cool one. Lincoln officials had reasoned that since the Seville was based on the GM NOVA (Chevy Nova, Olds Omega, Pontiac Ventura, Buick Apollo) body shell, it would be perfectly acceptable to base the Versailles on the Ford Granada/Mercury Monarch shell.

They failed to take into account, however, the extent to which Cadillac had differentiated the Seville from its cheaper brethren. Virtually nothing on the Seville obviously interchanged with any other GM compact, whereas the Versailles looked for all the world like a Granada with a Mark grille and a tire hump rather awkwardly grafted onto the back. The buyers stayed away in droves despite the fact that the Versailles was priced a couple of thousand dollars below the Seville.

Despite the Versailles disaster, Lincoln production reached an all-time

1977 Versailles.

record level of 191,355 units in 1977. Both Continental and Mark sales were way above the previous year. Final Continental production was 95,600, and final Mark V production reached 80,321. Versailles production for the remainder of the 1977 model run totaled just 15,434, a full 25 percent less than projected—and that proved to be the high point in the line's sad career.

After the activity of the previous year, 1978 was designed to be a year of relative quiet around the Lincoln factory. The Continental and Mark V shared a number of developments. The 400 cubic inch V8 introduced in 1977 was now

Top, 1977 Versailles interior; *bottom*, 1977 Versailles.

the standard engine on both lines, although the old 460 V8 could be special ordered on Continentals sold outside California and certain high altitude areas. A new electronic voltage regulator, a new maintenance free battery and an improved torque converter for the automatic transmission were other mechanical developments. Metallic exterior finishes were now of the clear-coat

Top, 1978 Continental Mark V interior; *bottom*, 1978 Continental.

type introduced on the 1977-1/2 Versailles. Clear acrylic enamel was applied over the regular color to increase visual depth. New options included wire wheels, an outside thermometer that was built into the base of the left-hand rear view mirror, and a 40-channel CB radio.

The Mark V story was limited to the usual array of luxury trim options of various descriptions. By far the most luxurious of these was the Diamond Jubilee Edition created to celebrate the 75th anniversary of the Ford Motor Company. This package, which retailed in the neighborhood of $8,000, was the most elaborate ever conceived for a production series Lincoln. It was available in two colors, diamond blue or jubilee gold, and the cars were completely color coordinated. Even exterior parts such as the vertical grille bars, bumper guards, and the rub strips, the cast aluminum wheels and the grille ornaments were finished to compliment the chosen color. Inside, individual front bucket seats were upholstered in luxury body cloth with fancy broadlace inserts. A padded, leather-covered console separated the two front seats and contained a storage compartment with a built-in umbrella. Padded leather and woodtone inserts were liberally distributed throughout the interior of the car. The keys even had woodtone inserts, and the owner's manual was leatherbound to match the interior, as was the leather-wrapped tool kit. The carpet was extra-thick 36-ounce Tiffany cut pile. The owner's initials were reproduced on the outside of the door and the opera windows contained Diamond Jubilee Edition script. There were many other special features, including, but by no means limited to, a special hood ornament and a padded rear deck bulge. In addition, many items that were optional on other Mark Vs were standard equipment on this model.

Overshadowed, but still very much alive, were the Designer Edition models. The Mark V Luxury Group Options were also still in the catalogue. They were all of the "mix and match" type and included Chaois, Cordovan, Wedgewood Blue, Dove Grey, Red/Rosé, Jade/Light Jade, and Gold Cream. As if that weren't enough, a new Carriage Roof option was also listed. This was an ersatz convertible top made of white vinyl.

A "Miles to Empty" fuel indicator was offered. It was a computer fuel monitoring device connected to a digital read-out on the instrument panel, and was an early version of the trip computer concept.

The Versailles was little altered for 1978. The 302 V8 was standard in all states, and a new light weight, high efficiency power steering pump and an Electronic Engine Control system were featured. It didn't do much good, as Versailles sales fell precipitously even over 1977's miserable total.

Lincoln production declined somewhat to 169,620 units in 1978. This number included 88,087 Continentals 72,602 Mark Vs and 8,931 Versailles.

By 1979, Lincoln was the last marque in the world still offering traditional American full-size luxury. Cadillac had downsized its model range in 1977 and 1979, and Chrysler made the switch in 1979. In 1980, the Lincolns were to be downsized like the rest. So in 1979, Lincoln had a market to itself.

In order to commemorate the passing of the big luxury car, Lincoln offered Collector Series models in both Continental and Mark V lines. Other features in common to the large Lincolns in 1979 included enlarged heater core inlets for better theft protection, the expanded use of woodtone appliqué on instrument panels and a new optional digital electronic AM/FM stereo radio with Quadrasonic 8-track tape deck. The 400 V8 was the only engine available.

The Collector's Series Continental was finished in midnight blue metallic, and continued a number of features introduced on the 1978 Diamond Jubilee Edition Mark V: gold bars in the grille, leather bound owner's manual and leather wrapped tool kit, an umbrella and a host of special features that were optional on other Continentals. Upholstery was midnight blue Kasman II luxury cloth.

The Williamsburg Town Car option was expanded to include seven two-tone exterior color schemes: silver/grey metallic, medium turquoise/dark turquoise, light champagne/dark champagne, gold/cream, cream/gold, cordovan metallic/crystal apricot metallic, and crystal apricot metallic/cordovan metallic. Interiors were in harmonizing velour.[1]

1979 Continental.

The Mark V also offered a Collector's Series model of similar description to the Continental version. Other than the color scheme, this model was a close continuation of the Diamond Jubilee Edition Mark V in most details. The Designer Series Mark Vs were also continued into the 1979 model run. The "mix and match" Luxury Group options were expanded again in 1979. The total availability was increased to nine groups, each of which offered a number of paint and trim possibilities: White, Crystal Blue, Wedgewood Blue, Dove Grey, Champagne, Gold/Cream, Turquoise, Red/Rosé and Cordovan.

The Versailles was also in for some revisions in 1979 in a desperate effort to jump start its flagging effort to compete with Cadillac's highly successful Seville. The biggest alteration was the roof. It was squared off considerably and, in the process, lengthened by eight inches. This was almost entirely cosmetic in nature. Although the rear door opening was increased somewhat, interior dimensions were virtually unchanged. Lincoln stated that the Versailles' list of standard equipment was the "most complete ever offered on a Ford Motor Company car,"[2] and included: coach lamps, vinyl half-roof padded rear deck lid, forged aluminum wheels, tinted glass, power windows, rear seat reading lamps, plus two others too numerous to list. An important new feature was the first use on an American car of halogen headlights. They, too, were standard equipment.

Lincoln production rose again in 1979, and to near record levels. The final

1979 Continental.

1979 Continental Mark V.

total for the model run—189,546—was only 1,809 units shy of the all-time Lincoln record in 1977, and this would have been another record year if the summer gasoline crisis of 1979 had not intervened to put an unexpected damper on luxury car sales. The Versailles, which had been a disappointment to the company, scored its biggest success in 1979. Production rose by 135 percent to 21,007 units.

The problem was complex. First, sluggish Pinto and Bobcat sales threatened Ford's corporate fuel economy average (CAFE) and Lincoln officials were forced to artificially restrict sales by raising prices. Secondly, the Iranian revolution, in late 1978 and early 1979, caused a disruption in gasoline supplies leading to long gas lines in the spring of 1979. When that happened, big car sales fell off the chart and Lincoln was dead in the water. The factory shut down early for the 1980 model changeover, but Lincoln-Mercury dealers were still trying to move unsold 1979 Lincolns well into the spring of 1980. A final total of 92,600 Continentals and 75,939 Mark Vs were built. It was a sad conclusion to a glorious decade.

Meanwhile, the situation in the auto industry was becoming more and more uncertain. Increasing (and sometimes contradictory) government regulations, inflation, recession, rising interest rates, and a continuation of the seemingly endless energy crises relentlessly took their toll. The market for big cars was further restrained by the poor retail value of used big cars. When past big car buyers went to the dealer to trade for the new, more efficient downsized models only to discover that the cars they owned were worth far less than anticipated, the result, in all too many cases, was "no sale."

Lincoln had little choice but to soldier on. Gail Halderman headed the 1980 Lincoln design team. His efforts were monitored by Eugene Bordinat, who had performed that function for twenty years. In May, 1980, Gordon MacKenzie was named to succeed Walter S. Walla as general manager.

The Halderman team was intent upon maintaining Lincoln's proven styling themes. Bodinat had stressed the need for continuity when he sought a way to pull Lincoln out of its doldrums back in the late 1950s. That philosophy had served Lincoln well and there seemed to be no reason to abandon it now. So, the 1980 Lincolns and Marks were styled much as in the past, but in a new, far more efficient package. Space efficiency was the key to the 1980 models. They had to do everything the 1979 models had done, only better and more economically.

The Mark series was expanded to include a four-door sedan for the first time. That was the good news. The bad news was that both were thinly disguised Town Cars/Coupes and shared virtually everything save minor trim details with their cheaper, less prestigious brethren. The 1980 Versailles was not changed in any major way, but nobody much cared. This was slated to be its final year, in any case. Ford management had learned the hard way that the

1979 Versailles.

Lincoln nameplate alone was not enough to sell cars; a model had to be perceived as being in the Lincoln class. They couldn't wait to see it go.

The 1980 models were announced just in time for a major national recession and a crushing rise in interest rates that saw the prime rate break 20 percent—two-and-a-half times the traditional level. Sales of big cars collapsed by the middle of the 1980 model year. The Cadillac De Villes and Fleetwoods suffered, too, so Lincoln was by no means alone in its misery, but the collapse of big Lincoln sales was significantly worse than that suffered by Cadillac. The absence of a competitive compact luxury car was clearly hurting, too; the Seville and Eldorado were all that were keeping Cadillac going. As 1980 deepened into 1981, however, there didn't appear to be much at all keeping Lincoln going.

Top, 1980 Continental interior; *bottom*, 1980 Continental.

The design of the 1980 series Lincolns and Marks was carefully crafted and there is every indication that the final result was just what Ford and Lincoln-Mercury management had wanted—which recalls the old saying about being careful what you wish for. While it definitely looked like a Lincoln, it was a fairly awkward example of the late 1970s "square" school of design prevalent at Ford. This style had first been seen in the successful 1977 Fairmont/Zephyr series compacts, but later reached the point of self-caricature in the disastrous Thunder-bird/Cougar models introduced for 1979. The 1980 series Lincolns and Marks weren't quite so bad, but they were far from well received in the marketplace—at least initially.

The long-awaited downsized Lincolns arrived on October 12, 1979—and Continental and Mark sales collapsed to virtual depression status. Only 74,908 were built during the 1980 run, down a staggering 60 percent from the year before, despite the fact that the cars themselves were quite good—perhaps the finest Lincolns ever built.

The real story for 1980 was engineering. The new Continental and Mark were smaller, lighter, and substantially more space efficient than the 1979 models they replaced. Over 800 pounds of weight was shed. The new models were approximately 14 inches shorter and nearly 2 inches narrower than before. And, yet, most interior dimensions were actually increased over 1979, some to a significant degree. The previously downsized Cadillac De Villes and Fleetwoods were also surpassed by Lincoln in every major interior dimension except one—and that one (front seat head room) was a tie. This was achieved despite the 4.1 inch shorter wheelbase of the Continentals.

The standard powerplant in 1980 was a reworked 302 cubic inch V8 fitted with fuel injection and Electronic Engine Control (EEC). This latter feature incorporated an on-board computer and seven sensors to monitor engine functions, including spark, air and fuel mixture, and exhaust gas recirculation. All of this resulted in fuel economy unheard-of in a gasoline-powered V8 in the Lincoln class. Realistic highway figures of 22–24 miles per gallon were possible. A 351 cubic inch V8 was optional. This engine included the Electronic Engine Control but passed up fuel injection in favor of the Variable Venturi two-barrel carburetor that had been pioneered on the Versailles in 1978. (The Electronic Engine Control had also been used for the first time on the Versailles as early as 1977 in California-bound models and became standard across the board in 1981 with this engine.)

Paired with the new Lincoln engines was a dramatically new transmission: the first automatic overdrive transmission made in America. This transmission featured a mechanical lock-up overdrive fourth gear that automatically en-

1980 Continental Mark IV.

gaged at approximately 40 miles per hour at minimum throttle, or at higher speeds under greater engine loads. It was a major contributor to the remarkable fuel efficiency of the new models.

Several intriguing new electronic options were listed. The Electronic Instrument Panel with Message Center involved an on-board computer using the latest microprocessor technology. Vehicle speed, time, day, date and fuel level were displayed on the instrument panel while the message center included a trip log computer providing, on demand, estimated time of arrival, average speed, distance to destination, and elapsed time and distance function. The Keyless Entry System permitted door-locking and unlocking, as well as decklid release, from the outside without use of a key. Entry was achieved by means of five push buttons on the driver's door connected to a minicomputer activated by the owner's special five-digit code. Both of these systems were optional on the Continental and standard on the Mark VI.

Additional technical features standard on the new Continental and Mark included halogen headlamps, P-metric radial-ply tires with reduced roll resistance and a "fluidic" windshield washer system with a single oscillating jet stream.

The most dramatic news in the model line-up was the addition of a Mark VI four-door sedan—the first (and only) four-door Mark. Most of the styling themes were carry-overs from the 1979 models, redone within the limitations of the new package. The Continental and Mark were really distinguished only by trim differences. The Mark had shuttered headlights and unique rear quarter panels, and the two-door body style sat on a 3 inch shorter wheelbase that it shared with the Mercury Marquis. One option available only on the Mark was special touring lamps, while Dual-Shade paints were optional only on the

Continental and Versailles. The latter option consisted of two-tone paint that separated lengthwise just below the belt-line.

The Continental was offered in two series: the standard Continental and the Continental Town Car/Coupe. The Collector's Series and Williamsburg options were dropped for 1980. The Mark was where the special trim action was to be found, being offered in standard, Signature and Designer series and in numerous luxury groups.

The Signature Series was the new top-of-the-line Mark. Every major comfort and convenience feature was standard. The Designer Series was available, as in 1979, in Pucci, Bill Blass, Givenchy, and Cartier editions, although the colors and trims in each underwent the customary annual revisions.

The Versailles was continued for 1980 in essentially unchanged form.

The 1980 Continental and Mark were well received by the motoring press. *Motor Trend* magazine said of the Mark VI:

> Its all-new frame, body, suspension, steering, brakes and transmission are part of the car's incredibly luxurious nature . . . With overdrive, the engine runs at about 1800 rpm at 60 mph, eliminating the largest source of noise and

1980 Versailles.

pushing engine wear and highway mileage to new levels . . .The Mark VI is a design awash in the technology of metals, materials and electronics, which has made it a good deal more space- and fuel-efficient than its domestic competition.[3]

In a similar vein, *Car and Driver* magazine reported:

Lincoln-Mercury did an excellent job of restating the Lincoln styling theme on these smaller canvases . . . It almost goes without saying that the new Lincolns are still low-effort, low-feel, velour-lined rolling palaces—as smooth as good brandy and as quiet as a library at midnight.[4]

Despite their newness and inherent worth, the 1980 Lincolns were unable to compensate for a collapsing luxury car market and poorly received styling. Of the 74,908 cars produced during the 1980 model run, 38,891 were Marks, 31,233 were Continentals and an almost invisible 4,784 were Versailles.

The 1981 Lincolns were pretty much a repeat of the 1980 line-up. Nameplates were moved around a bit, most notably the change in designation of the standard Lincolns from Continental to Town Car in anticipation of the downsized 1982 Continental. The Versailles, as planned, was deleted from the catalogue. The Lincoln Continental Mark VI became simply the Continental Mark VI.

1981 Continental Mark VI.

There were the usual color and trim changes. Puncture-resistant wide whitewall tires were a new option. In addition, the Mark VI featured an instantaneous fuel economy display function on the electronic instrument panel, a new mix mode for the automatic temperature control system that permitted a division of air flow between the windshield and the passengers' feet, a remote control decklid release, power door locks, a remote control mirror, intermittent wipers, speed control and a tilt steering wheel. Wire wheels became standard on the Signature Series.

There were few substantive engineering changes. The most notable one was the deletion of the 351 cubic inch engine.

Sales, unfortunately, continued to deteriorate. The country was in the grips of the worst recession in the postwar period and combined Lincoln production slumped to 69,537, a 7 percent decline over even 1980's depressed totals. Production bottomed out at a level barely one-third the record pace of 1979. Fortunately, the worst was over.

The big news in 1982 was the downsized replacement for the unlamented Versailles, which had been dropped at the end of the 1980 model run (an event that was probably not widely noticed). The replacement was based on the Fairmont/Mustang platform and bore Lincoln's most treasured nameplate: Continental. If this seems odd, it must be remembered that, in the 1980–81 time frame in which the car was brought to completion, it was widely accepted that large cars of the Town Car genre were dinosaurs doomed to extinction. They were already selling poorly and gasoline prices, expected to rise to perhaps $3 a gallon by the mid-1980s, were sure to finish them off. Thus, the Continental nameplate was taken off the big cars and given to the Versailles because, a), the Versailles name was already discredited, and, b), it was assumed that this size car would be the mainstay of the Lincoln fleet by the end of the decade, if not sooner.

The 1982 Continental was a first-class effort throughout and showed that Ford had learned its marketing lessons from the Versailles program. It was actually only marginally lighter than the Town Car (by about 6 percent), but substantially smaller on its 108.5 inch wheelbase. Still, it looked fuel efficient, and that was probably deemed sufficient for most Lincoln prospects.

The looks were also memorable for being of the short-lived "razorback" school of design. Developed by Hooper in England in the 1940s, the pronounced downward curve of the beltline met a dramatic concave downward sweep at the rear window and combined to give a racy look (and a characteristic trunk bulge) to the rather boxy Rolls-Royce of the day. Cadillac revived the style when it wanted a "classic" look for its second generation 1980 Seville.

Top, 1982 Continental; *bottom*, 1982 Mark VI.

Chrysler picked it up for the last-gasp Imperial coupe built in very small numbers between 1981 and 1983, and Lincoln joined the group with the 1982 Continental.

Designers at all three companies experienced problems in translating the razorback onto the lower and wider proportions of contemporary cars. Cadillac effected the purest evocation of the style in 1980, then, flinching in the face of tepid public response, tried to de-emphasize the trunk bulge with a wide beltline molding after 1981. The Continental went Cadillac one better with body sculpturing that emphasized the beltline even more. The result on both cars was an odd-looking convex beltline curve that made them look hunched in the middle, rather like a cat with its back up. Chrysler designers didn't bother with the beltline curve at all, but still ended up with a surprisingly pleasing result that probably would have been even more impressive in a four-door configuration. Around Chrysler, the failure of the Imperial was widely blamed on the decision to go with a coupe body style.

None of the three cars was notably successful—even the addition of a powder-blue "Frank Sinatra Edition" to the Imperial line, complete with no less than 16 cassette tapes recorded by Old Blue Eyes himself, could spur sales there—but the Continental came off best overall, at least commercially.

Sitting on a 108.5 inch wheelbase, the new model was nearly nine inches shorter than the Town Car and a foot-and-a-half shorter overall. Inside, it was done up in the best Lincoln fashion, complete with an elaborate rendering of Lincoln's touted electronic instrument panel. This was no low-buck pretender like the Cadillac Cimarron introduced the same year. The Continental competed against the Seville and was priced accordingly: $21,302 for the base model, with Signature and Givenchy editions pushing the tab even higher.

Power was supplied by the proven Ford 5.0-liter V8, while a 3.8-liter V6 was available for the economy-minded. This latter engine actually did little to improve gas mileage—the Continental's nearly two-ton weight precluded real fuel economy—but Lincoln wanted a counter to the six-cylinder and diesel engine options being offered by Cadillac. The six never sold well, however, and was quietly dropped after the initial model run. The Continental also featured nitrogen-pressurized shocks. Borrowed from Ford Europe, they were the first shock absorbers of the type to be used on any American car. Continental options included just about anything available on Town Car or Mark models.

The Continental received mostly noncommittal revues from the buff magazines. In a head-to-head comparison test with the Seville, *Motor Trend* observed that the Continental "proved more receptive to spirited motoring" but found the Seville to be the more "opulent" car. The magazine also noted:

> Lincoln-Mercury looks upon the Continental as a conquest vehicle. By slanting it toward a bit younger, more adventurous buyer, L-M hopes to snare a few of the borderline free spirits who can often be seen lurking about Cadillac dealerships.[5]

If this was true, Ford management must have been sorely disappointed.

Deleted for 1982 was the Town Coupe, the two-door version of the Town Car. It had never sold well and Town Car series sales rose despite its absence. The Town Car received increased emphasis with a new Cartier Designer Series. The Mark VI was therefore down to only two Designer models: Pucci and Bill Blass (the Givenchy edition had gone to the new Continental). A couple of new roof treatments were listed as Mark options, however—the Specialty Coach Roof (rear half only) and Specialty Full Roof.

Projected production for the Continental—40,000 for the 1982 run—was missed by a wide margin: only 23,908 were built, but it was still about 20 percent better than the Seville's performance that year. Town Car production rose modestly to 35,069, while the Mark VI fell to 26,336. Overall Lincoln production—85,313—was nonetheless up 22 percent over 1981's dreadful pace and

Top, 1983 Continental interior; *bottom*, 1983 Continental.

represented the first heartening news in several seasons. Lincoln was back from the dead—barely.

Changes for 1983 were mostly limited to refinements in trim details. Ford Motor Company as part of its quality drive had taken to reserving major changes for new product launches. The idea was that getting it right the first time was a far better long-term strategy than improving it as you went along. It seemed to be working for by this time Ford was gaining a reputation with the public as America's highest-quality automobile producer—a view that was an especial asset to Lincoln.

For 1983, a Valentino Designer Series was added to the Continental, and vinyl roof options continued to be the focus of the development efforts devoted to the Town Car and Mark VI. An optional anti-theft alarm system was also offered. On the engineering front, the Continental's V6 engine option was deleted, while the 5.0-liter V8 was improved by the addition of fuel injection.

Sales showed a marked upswing—refreshing news at last. All of the improvement came with the big cars, though. Town Car production jumped 52 percent to 53,381 and Mark VI production rose 17 percent to 30,856. Some of this was due to general improvement in the nation's economic picture, but the Town Car was beginning to feel the start of the big car boom that was to take place in the middle years of the decade. In contrast, production of the Continental—the series that was supposed to be the salvation of Lincoln in the 1980s—slumped 30 percent to 16, 831. Still, it was an encouraging year overall, with Lincoln production creeping past the century mark for the first time since 1979.

The truly cosmic news at Lincoln in 1984 was the advent of the entirely redesigned Mark VII. This proved to be the model that set Lincoln in a new direction toward building international-type luxury cars that could excite serious enthusiasts and, in so doing, made history as the first American luxury maker to field a car that could effectively compete in this important new market segment.

Still, the Mark VII came in two flavors designed to appeal to two very different types of buyers. The first was the standard Mark VII, which catered to the traditional Mark customer with a comparatively squishy ride, plastic wood trim inside and acres of velour upholstery. Designer editions of this first type were also provided through the participation of Bill Blass and Gianni Versace.

The second type was the Mark VII LSC (for "luxury sport coupe") which did away with the velour and wood, substituting leather-covered multi-adjustable seats and a chassis tuned for serious performance driving. Bucket seats and a full-length console were standard in both versions. The signature

1983 Town Car.

tire bulge at the back, also standard, irritated many enthusiasts who tended to forgive all as soon as they climbed behind the wheel. As a driver's car, the LSC was a revelation.

Both Mark VII models featured an industry first: electronic air suspension controlled by an on-board microcomputer. It used Goodyear air springs. Lincoln also claimed the first fully integrated flush-mounted road lighting system, which featured European-style halogen headlamps. Power for both Marks came from Ford's 5.0-liter V8 and a new German-built ZF four-speed automatic overdrive transmission. A BMW-built 2.4-liter turbo-diesel was offered for a short time—the duration being severely curtailed by the absence of paying customers. Diesel technology had become a dead letter with American car buyers by this point.

Mark VII LSC equipment included an impressive array of performance items: heavy-duty front and rear stabilizers, revised spring rates, quick-ratio steering, a performance rear axle, high performance Goodyear tires, fog lamps, leather (or leather-and-cloth) upholstery, and leather-covered console armrest, gearshift handle, and steering wheel. Carpeting and trunk finishing was also upgraded.

1984 Mark VII.

The 1984 Marks boasted a then-remarkable 0.38 drag coefficient. They were significantly more efficient than their predecessors in other ways, too. The Mark VII was 350 pounds lighter, 13 inches shorter and 1.5 inches lower. It was based on the Thunderbird/Cougar platform (also used by the Continental). The body was redesigned for the Mark VII, but was regarded by many prospects as being far too close in appearance to its less expensive cousins. In truth, there was very little visible inside or out that was common between the three lines, but all were examples of Ford's new "aero" school of design and shared a marked family resemblance as a result.

The enthusiast press was truly excited about the Mark VII LSC. *Motor Trend* said:

> The LSC version has got to be Ford's most daring move of the decade. In concept and execution, [it] has been redefined into something other than a luxury boat and has entered territory previously held by German sturmwagens.[6]

Car and Driver wrote:

> Certain to mystify Lincoln's traditional constituency, the LSC is tailored to the requirements of wealthy, discriminating enthusiasts (read, Mercedes-Benz buyers). Knee-jerk sporty-car types won't believe that, but it's true. This latest version is swift and sure-footed and will look considerably more at home cruising the autobahn than the red-light district of your home town. The old Mark has come a long way.[7]

Unfortunately, dealers were able to keep the Mark VII in stock. A total of 33,344 were built during the 1984 model run, significantly shy of the 45,000 projected. Of this number, perhaps 2,300 were diesels.

Despite its virtues (or possibly because of them), the Mark VII was the third consecutive Lincoln product launch that had been a serious disappointment. Worse, Mark VII production fell far below the 77,806 Cadillac Eldorados built that year. Still, there was an underlying satisfaction around the company; Lincoln-Mercury knew it had built an extraordinary car.

The Mark VII's main failing may have been that it stretched the envelope too far for its existing customer base. But, it had also earned new respect for Lincoln from enthusiasts, import fanciers and younger people who would be driving the luxury market in the 1990s and beyond. In the final analysis, the Mark VII was a modest commercial failure, but an honorable one that significantly advanced Lincoln's prospects in the long run.

There was no question, however, about one Lincoln failure in this period: the turbo-diesel offered on the Mark VII in 1984. The fact that Lincoln ever offered a diesel will no doubt come as a revelation to many and that should provide an indication of just how few were sold. The diesel program was another product of the early-1980s' obsession with fuel efficiency. And, too, it must be remembered that Cadillac was doing a big business in diesels in the 1978–81 period when 1984 product plans were being made. Cadillac officials at one time were projecting that 80 percent or more of their cars would be diesels by 1985.

Top, 1984 Mark VII LSC interior; *bottom*, 1984 Mark VII LSC.

Ford didn't have a diesel, so a deal was struck with BMW to import a six-cylinder turbo-diesel for Lincoln. Projections were for 8,000–10,000 units in 1984. Actual numbers are hard to come by, but it appears that about 2,300 Mark VIIs and perhaps 1,500 Continentals were fitted before the program collapsed of its own dead weight. They were good cars, but the diesel market had evaporated by 1984. This collapse left GM with hundreds of thousands of disgruntled owners and lots of very expensive and very useless plant capacity, while Ford was stuck with a lifetime supply of replacement engines. Of the two, Ford got the better of the bargain by far.

The Continental benefited from a raft of modifications and refinements in 1984. Most notable among them were: electronic air suspension, expanded electronic display instrument panel functions including color coded warning lights (yellow for "caution," red for "stop"), revised front end styling, and upgraded soft trim on the interior. One more was the relocation of the horn button from the directional signal stalk to the steering wheel hub. In the early 1980s, Ford had briefly begun switching models over to the stalk-activated horn system until customer complaints forced a reversion to the traditional location.

The Town Car offered a few changes, including gas-pressurized shocks and an optional power decklid pulldown. This latter item had been a great favorite with Cadillac owners since the late 1960s.

The Lincoln product book in 1984 noted that "the plentiful gasoline supply has helped Lincoln sales boom in recent months." Indeed. On top of the 52 percent gain registered in 1983, Town Car sales were to see another whopping 76 percent increase in 1984. The 93,622 Town Cars built helped mightily to push total Lincoln production in 1984 to 157,434. It was the fourth best year in Lincoln history and only about 18 percent below the all-time record in 1977.

Lincoln was back in the game.

CHAPTER TEN

This teaser shot of the 1993 Mark VIII appeared in the 1992 Lincoln sales brochure. If only the actual car had been as interesting . . .

Soaring: 1985–99

THE JAPANESE INVASION of the late 1970s, combined with the fuel crisis and recession sparked by the Iranian revolution in 1979, sent Detroit into a tailspin. Chrysler teetered on the brink of bankruptcy, while Ford Motor Company lost billions and looked as if it might follow suit. The situation was saved in Dearborn by a top-to-bottom reorganization in the early 1980s, a key part of which was remaking the company into a leader in quality engineering and manufacturing.

In the wake of the reorganization, Lincoln led Ford Motor Company's quest for higher standards—recognized both by industry insiders and by the buying public. That no doubt served to bolster Lincoln sales in this period, together with aggressive sales to fleet outlets: rental car companies, business leases, etc. (For a period of several years in the early 1980s, the Town Car was reduced to existing mostly as a fleet vehicle for Ford.) What really catapulted the Town Car to sales success, however, were failures at Cadillac.

Lincoln benefited mightily from the disturbing drop in Cadillac quality in the early 1980s. Cadillac's notorious "V8-6-4" modular displacement engine, introduced in 1981 as an effort to improve fuel economy, was quickly dropped, but not before it severely tarnished Cadillac's once sterling reputation for engineering excellence. GM's wretched diesel engine produced further buyer alienation. Even though Cadillac had nothing directly to do with the diesel's engineering, tens of thousands were sold to Cadillac customers—many of whom left the GM fold for good as a consequence. Another of Cadillac's answers to the repeated fuel crises of the era appeared in 1982 in the form of the compact Cimarron. Based all-too-obviously on the low-buck Chevrolet Cavalier, the Cimarron made every mistake Lincoln had made with the ill-fated Versailles—only more so—and further diluted Cadillac's prestige.

The coup de grace for Cadillac's image, however, came in 1985 with its down-sized, front-drive DeVille/Fleetwood models. They arrived just as the market for traditional-size luxury cars was rebounding. Ford, which simply didn't have the money to develop a new Lincoln Town Car during this period, was forced to stick with the 1980-series product. That "strategy"—such as it was—proved to be a gold mine when the big car boom returned. A pleasant face-lift of the Town Car in 1985 smoothed out most of the awkward lines in the 1980 design and helped spur things along.

Moreover, the face-lift was magnificently timed because of Cadillac's disastrous decision to completely de-emphasize its big rear-drive Brougham series when the smaller, front-drive DeVilles and Fleetwoods were first announced. This pushed many long-time Cadillac buyers over to Lincoln in the mistaken belief that Cadillac no longer offered a traditional-size luxury sedan, and,

1985 Town Car.

largely as a consequence, Town Car production soared from a pathetic 32,839 units in 1981 to 119,878 by 1985. By 1988, overall Lincoln production would reach 280,659 units—72 percent of them Town Cars—and Cadillac would be in the toughest fight it had known in half-a-century.

Lincoln also scored a major coup in 1985 with one of the most talked about television commercials of the era. A rare example of "attack" advertising that really worked, it was created to cash in on problems Cadillac was having with consumer acceptance of their down-sized, front-drive DeVille/Fleetwood models introduced for 1985. The television commercial showed an elegant couple leaving a posh restaurant. They ask the valet for their Cadillac, only to be offered a look-alike Olds 98 which another elegantly dressed couple then confuses for their Buick, and so on, until a Lincoln Town Car pulls up and yet another elegant couple get in, obviously proud of their truly distinguished automobile. This commercial was devastatingly effective and quickly achieved critical mass. Everyone from stand-up comics to comic strip artists did take-offs. Needless to say, this did Lincoln's prime competitor no good at all in a market segment where distinction has always been one of the main buying motivations, while, at the same time, positioning the Town Car as a unique, non-look-alike alternative.

As noted, for 1985 the Town Car was mildly redesigned. The changes were more than skin deep, however, and involved welcome refinements throughout

1985 Continental.

the series. A major development was the automatic load-leveling suspension option designed to keep a Town Car on an even keel even when fully loaded. The system worked by means of adjustable rear shocks controlled by an electronic sensor. It was particularly suited to Town Car owners who traveled, as a large percentage of them did, and was an overdue example of playing catch-up with Cadillac, which had offered a similar system for many years.

A couple of standard equipment changes made in response to customer demand included use of a single key for all locks and removal of the horn button from the directional signal stalk to the steering wheel hub. Other than that, changes were mostly ones of color and trim, but the overall result was a far more appealing product.

Thomas J. Wagner arrived in the general manager's office just in time to bask in all this good news. Town Car production rose another 28 percent to 119,878 cars for the model run. In contrast, Continental and Mark VII production slipped—to 28,253 and a depressing 18,355, respectively—but overall Lincoln production hit a new high for the decade: 166,486.

Despite their slip in sales, there were a couple of significant developments on the Continental and Mark VII. One was anti-lock brakes, which were made standard on Designer Series models and on the LSC. This was one of the first American applications of this important technology. The LSC also benefitted from a new, high-output version of the 5.0-liter engine delivering

1986 Mark VII.

165 horsepower (versus 140 for the standard engine), as well as new fully adjustable, articulated seats.

The following year, 1986, was one of rest following the major product developments of the two previous seasons. All lines received refinements, but there were no startling developments either in the products or in their reception, with production remaining steady at 1985's fast pace.

Across the line, the major developments were the addition of multi-port electronic fuel injection to the 5.0-liter V8—boosting rated horsepower from 140 to 150 for the standard engine and to 200 for the high-output version—and the advent of Ford's superlative JBL sound system as an option. This latter item won rave reviews from audiophiles and put Lincoln at the front rank in the industry in terms of the quality of its audio systems. Also this year, the center high-mounted stop lights (CHMSL, pronounced "chim-sell") became standard on all cars sold in America.

In addition, anti-lock brakes were made standard on all Continental and Mark VII models. The Mark VII LSC also benefitted from suspension modifications that improved its already superb ride and handling characteristics. Finally, the Valentino (Continental) and Versace (Mark VII) Designer Series models were dropped.

If 1986 was a year of rest at Lincoln, 1987 was a year of slumber. Product developments were confined to the most minor revisions, mostly in the availabil-

1986 Town Car.

Top, 1987 Continental; *bottom*, 1987 Town Car Sail America Commemorative Edition.

ity of optional equipment. A compact disc player was available on the Town Car for the first time, while all models received upgraded corrosion protection.

Sales were down a bit for the model run in 1987 partly because revised 1988 designated Town Car and Mark VII models were introduced early in the calendar year. Overall production dipped to 109,366, including 76,483 Town Cars, 15,286 Mark VIIs, and 17,597 Continentals. It was destined to be a momentary dip, however, as sales came roaring back in 1988.

A completely new Continental was introduced in 1988. Based on the wildly successful Taurus/Sable platform, the new Continental was a big hit, too. In fact, sales consistently outran production throughout the model year—the first time in many a year Ford had faced that particular problem with a Lincoln series—leaving would-be buyers and Lincoln-Mercury dealers screaming for cars.

The 1988 Continental was the first front-wheel-drive Lincoln. Power was provided by a 3.8-liter V6, while anti-lock brakes were standard. This meant that the Continental stopped somewhat better than it went, for the V6 was widely criticized for its unexciting acceleration. That was about the only criticism leveled at the new line, though. With rack-and-pinion steering and four-wheel independent air suspension, it rode and handled much like a Mark VII LSC. Two models were listed: the standard Continental and the Signature Series.

Motor Trend loved the new Continental:

> The most advanced, best-engineered, best-driving Lincoln ever built. Also arguably the best-looking Lincoln sedan in quite a few years. Just another fine example of Ford Motor Company going its own way, the customer's way.[1]

In a syndicated review that appeared in *Palm Beach Illustrated*, the author generally concurred and added:

> Noticeably Teutonic in its styling, the Continental is clearly aimed at both Cadillac and at the European imported luxury sedans. The car is handsome and properly sybaritic. The 3.8-liter V6 is smooth and flexible, even though it could stand a little more punch. Overall, the Continental is more than competitive with similar six-cylinder luxury sedans, including some foreign jobs costing thousands more.[2]

The 1988 Town Car and Mark VII were announced in March, 1987, and featured new grilles and trim in both instances. The JBL sound system was also added to the Mark VII options list and the high-output engine was made

1988 Mark VII LSC.

standard throughout the line. The line itself was reduced to two models: the Bill Blass Designer Series and the LSC. The Town Car line-up remained as before, with standard, Signature and Cartier Designer models.

It turned out to be the best year in Lincoln history and, by the time the dust settled, a total of 280,659 Lincolns had been built. This represented a 157 percent increase over 1987—but, of course, the 1987 model year had been an abbreviated one, so the results weren't quite as astonishing as they seemed. Of the grand total, 201,113 were Town Cars—which, by itself, would have been an overall Lincoln record—plus 38,259 Mark VIIs and 41,287 Continentals. A final piece of news in 1988 was a change in leadership. Ross Roberts replaced Thomas J. Wagner as general manager.

Top, 1988 Continental interior; *bottom,* 1989 Continental.

In retrospect, the 1988-series Continental was a mistake on a couple of levels. One problem was that it just wasn't good enough to be a Lincoln. The Taurus platform was all-too evident and the car was plagued with quality problems that seriously damaged its reputation over time. The bigger failure, though, was strategic, and to understand that a little history is in order.

Across the water, Europeans had been building small luxury cars for years. European tax laws, traffic conditions, and fuel prices all mandated cars that were really too small for mass American tastes in the expansive 1950s and 1960s. Even cars of the four-seater T-Bird genre, while trending in the right direction, were huge and monstrously inefficient by prevailing European standards. Then came the 1970s and a number of factors interacted to progressively merge the European and American concepts and accelerate the trend toward a common international luxury car type.

Increasing affluence in Europe caused luxury car buyers over there to demand greater size, comfort, and power. Here in America, the fuel scares of 1973 and 1979 brought about a fundamental rethinking of efficiency standards, while the growing importance of the "baby boom" generation—a demographic group weaned on the high performance and sporty cars of the 1960s (Mustangs, GTOs, etc.)—prompted greater attention to non-traditional luxury car traits such as handling and performance. As a result of all these factors, European luxury rigs such as Mercedes-Benz got bigger and fancier, while American luxury car manufacturers (i.e., Cadillac and Lincoln) began to offer more efficiently sized and sportier vehicles. Still, the domestic manufacturers were slow to appreciate the shift in this segment despite the potential for the lush profits it offered.

Cadillac was the first to seem to appreciate the challenge and its initial effort was promising. The 1976 Seville was well-conceived, solidly successful, and even had a modicum of success in European markets. The next generation of the Seville (1980) and the related Eldorado (1979), however, failed to build on the Seville's initial success, while the third generation, introduced for 1986 for both Seville and Eldorado, was calamitous and represented the low point of Cadillac's near-collapse as a serious luxury car producer in the mid-1980s.

The 1986 "E/K" personal cars (Buick Riviera, Olds Toronado, and Cadillac Eldorado/Seville) were tremendous disappointments, both aesthetically and commercially. At Cadillac, the Eldorado received an emergency restyling for 1988, while the Seville was drastically reworked to try to render it at least marginally competitive. The most interesting result of this effort was the Seville STS high-performance sedan announced in 1988, but it was still an example of trying to make a silk purse out of a sow's ear. Quality control problems also plagued early examples of the E/K series. It wasn't until the introduction of another new Seville for the 1992 model year—arguably the most important new Cadillac announced in a generation—that Cadillac at last began to build a car widely perceived as a world-class effort.

Lincoln was the first American manufacturer to really score in this emerging international-size segment, although it took two misfires to hit the target. Lincoln rushed its compact Versailles to completion in the spring of 1977 in what turned out to be a major failure in "packaging" (to borrow a bit of design jargon). The successor to the Versailles, the compact Continental introduced in 1982, was far better, but Lincoln's first big success was with its remarkable Mark VII LSC introduced in 1984. It was the "hot rod" Lincoln reborn and perfectly embodied the blending of European size and appointments with the "baby boomer" approach to handling and performance.

As the 1980s drew on, and after numerous fits and starts, the basic outlines of the new international-type luxury car began to gel. Available in either sport sedan or sport coupe configurations, the car has a wheelbase of around 110 inches, an overall length of around 200 inches, and is powered by a V8 of around 4.5 liters in displacement. Prices start (as this is written) at about $40,000 and run on up into the stratosphere from there, although the most popular models fall into the $40,000 to $60,000 category.

The truly momentous news in the latter part of the 1980s, however, occurred when the Japanese manufacturers, forced out of the entry-level segment by the Koreans, cast a greedy eye toward the other end of the price scale and entered the fray with highly competitive luxury models of their own. The luxury class was the only market segment the Japanese had failed to crack and the Lexus LS 400 sedan (from Toyota) and the Infiniti Q45 sedan (from Nissan), both announced in 1990, fit almost exactly the new international specs. The Lexus, in particular, sent designers, engineers, and marketing mavens at luxury car companies all over the world rushing back to their drawing boards.

Suddenly, a segment that didn't even exist in 1975 had become the fastest growing and most hotly contested part of the luxury market. Any manufacturer who wanted to be taken seriously as a luxury car producer in the 1990s had to be competitive.

In retrospect, it is likely that Lincoln made a major strategic mistake with the conceptualization of the 1988 Continental, the second generation "little" Continental (or the third generation Versailles, if one wishes). Ford had the ready capability of choosing one of two very different directions, for there were two distinctly different platforms available. The first was the existing

1982–87 Continental rear-drive platform which also served as the basis for the Mark VII.

The second platform was the profoundly successful six-cylinder, front-drive Taurus/Sable platform, first introduced for the 1986 model year. The Ford Taurus and Mercury Sable were the cars that set the standard in domestic mass-market family cars and that really launched Ford Motor Company into its roaring momentum of the late 1980s. It was this platform that was chosen for the 1988 Continental. This is not, perhaps, surprising given the focus of the company at the time—to say nothing of the public reception accorded the Taurus and Sable in contrast to the disappointing reception accorded the Mark VII LSC.

The Taurus/Sable platform resulted in a Continental that was very well received, at least initially, but one wonders how the contemporary history of Lincoln—and of the domestic luxury car—might have been changed had the first option been chosen. In the rear-drive, V8-powered Mark VII platform, Lincoln possessed a proven design that could easily have been developed into a potent four-door sedan almost exactly fitting the description of the international class of luxury sedan fated to burst forth at almost the exact moment the 1988 Continental was introduced. Think of a four-door Mark VII LSC with styling done in the general fashion of the 1988 Continental and the missed potential becomes clear.

Be that as it may, 1989 was another year remarkable for its inactivity at Lincoln. Throughout the 1980s, as it rebuilt itself as a quality company, Ford tended to concentrate its efforts on its new models, engineering and designing them to the nth degree to make sure they were as perfect as they could be when they were introduced. The other side of this coin, however, was that once a model was announced it tended to be left pretty much alone, sometimes for years, with only detail refinements to denote model years. If there were no major product launches for a particular brand in a given year, there was often little to report. So it was with Lincoln in 1989.

The Town Car added a Gucci Designer Series model, while the Mark VII remained virtually unaltered. Curiously, the Continental, which had been all-new in 1988, received most of the changes, although nearly all of them were minor adjustments made to refine the product in direct response to customer complaints. Front seat travel was increased, for example. Concerns about the Continental's power (or, more properly, the lack thereof) were addressed in several ways: sequential multi-port fuel injection was added to the 3.8-liter engine, throttle shift speeds were modified, and the transaxle's final drive ratio was upped from 3.19:1 to 3.37:1. Lack of interior storage space had been noted in many published 1988 Continental road tests, so map pockets were added for 1989. As *Motor Trend* had earlier observed, Ford was now determined to do things the customer's way.

The only major change to the Continental was the addition of driver and passenger side air bags as standard. This was one of the very first dual air bag applications offered in any American car and required the redesign of the instrument panel fascia and steering wheel hub.

Sales dropped somewhat in 1989 from 1988's heady pace, but the year was still the second best in Lincoln history. The Town Car, which was nearing the end of its current generation, fell to 128,533, and the Mark VII fell more modestly to 29,658. The Continental, on the other hand, soared to 57,775 as supply at last rose to meet demand.

Since 1939, Lincolns had been the presidential cars of choice. That changed when President Reagan took office in 1981. For a time, Ford Motor Company and General Motors unofficially divided up the responsibility involved in producing presidential parade cars, most likely due to the enormous costs in complying with contemporary specifications. GM supplied the 1984 Cadillac parade car used during most of the Reagan era. In 1989, a new Lincoln parade car was delivered for the inauguration of George Bush. Then, a 1993 Cadillac was delivered just in time for the swearing-in of his successor, Bill Clinton, and a 2001 Cadillac was delivered for the inauguration of Clinton's successor, George W. Bush.

The George H. W. Bush Lincoln, designed and built in Ford's Advanced Vehicle Development facility in Dearborn Heights, Michigan, was in the planning stages for nearly five years. Actual construction took just under three years

1989 presidential limousine.

to complete. The vehicle was armored by O'Hara-Hess & Eisenhardt Armoring Company in Cincinnati, Ohio.

The 1989 parade car, as delivered, was two-and-a-half inches higher than a standard Town Car, and rode on a 162-inch wheelbase. Finished in midnight black clearcoat paint, the car featured a shadow-blue cloth-and-leather interior. As has been the case with other presidential vehicles in modern times, details concerning the most interesting features of the car were never released. Even the vehicle weight was classified.

If Bush Forty-One had just waited a year, he could have had the most successful new Lincoln model of the era.[3] While the concept behind the 1988 Continental can be debated, there would appear to be no question that Lincoln scored a direct hit—strategically and commercially—with its next new product line: the completely redesigned 1990 Town Car. Fashioned to cater to the traditional luxury car buyer, the new Town Car revealed a great deal about Lincoln's contemporary strategic thinking. The four main design objectives for the new series were: 1) keep it American, 2) give it a contemporary look, 3) retain the Town Car package and size, and 4) retain the Town Car image.

Armed with the knowledge that the "baby boom" generation was inevitably becoming older and more affluent, Lincoln sought to create a luxury car that would maintain the Town Car's enviable reputation for size and luxury, yet add to it more youthful attributes sure to be valued by the next generation of luxury car buyers, such as efficiency, performance, and handling. The 1990 Town Car, for example, had a shape that was the result of extensive wind tunnel testing and was much more aerodynamic than its predecessor. It even utilized exotic design tricks, such as flush-mounted side window glass. Fuel economy was significantly improved as a result, as was the reduction in wind noise. The 1990 Town Car was so silent at highway speeds it practically redefined the term, and it got even quieter in 1991 with the advent of the 4.6-liter "modular" V8.

Suspension modifications also significantly improved the Town Car's stability, particularly on poor roads, without exacting any penalty from the whipped-cream-smooth ride for which this car had become famous. These included speed-sensitive, variable-assist power steering, a rear air spring load-leveling system, and a complete suspension redesign. The result was a Town Car that maintained the billowy ride for which the line had become famous, but for the first time it also delivered respectable handling.

Largely on the strength of the Town Car's soaring popularity in the late 1980s, Lincoln shaved Cadillac's once untouchable lead in sales from a margin of three-to-one to near parity. In June, 1990, Lincoln nearly out-sold

Cadillac nationally for the first time in history. Although this proved to be an anomaly, it did serve to give dramatic indication of how close the contest in luxury car sales had become.

In a review of the 1990 Town Car published in *Palm Springs Life*, the author reported:

> While Cadillac has been struggling to correct its marketing mistakes, restyling and stretching its DeVilles almost annually in an effort to improve their appeal, the Lincoln Town Car has taken on an air of prosperous permanence. It has become one of those oh-so-familiar cars that seem always to have been there so, naturally, we assume it always will be. Life does not work that way, though, and it was inevitable that the Town Car would one day be replaced. That day is at hand. The new and very much improved 1990 Town Car looks different and is different. Very different. The old Town Car had all the aerodynamics of a billboard.
>
> The new model has a much slipperier shape and looks like a Lincoln, but in a more contemporary and pleasing style, and presents far less physical resistance to the elements. The old Town Car was quiet, but the new one is so silent at highway speeds it practically redefines the term.
>
> Suspension modifications have also significantly improved the Town Car's stability, particularly on poor roads, without exacting any penalty from the whipped-cream-smooth ride for which this car has become famous.
>
> So, dramatically new, yet comfortingly familiar, the 1990 Town Car achieves the seemingly impossible. It has changed almost everything about the old model without sacrificing the old feel. If you loved the old Town Car, the odds are excellent that you will love this one, too.[4]

1990 Town Car.

The model line-up was also the same as before, with base, Signature and Cartier Designer Series models offered. In other developments for 1990, both Continental and Mark VII lines sported new grilles and exterior trim in an effort to freshen their appearance. The Mark VII also benefitted from a revised instrument panel and the addition of a driver-side air bag. On the LSC, attractive new BBS road wheels were made standard.

Lincoln sales improved throughout 1990 and ended with the second best year in the make's history: 233,730 cars, in all. The new Town Car led the field with 147,160 units—a 14 percent increase—while the Mark VII dipped to 22,313 and the Continental continued to gain favor, posting an 18 percent increase to 64,257 cars.

In general, 1991 was a year of consolidation of the gains Lincoln had made with its highly successful Town Car and Continental redesigns. The man assigned to monitor that was Lincoln-Mercury's new general manager, Lee R. Miskowski. The Town Car completed its metamorphosis with a new engine and a revised chassis. Meanwhile, sales of the Mark VII—then in its eighth year—began to languish noticeably.

The heart of the final go-'round for the Town Car was the new 4.6-liter modular V8 engine. Rated at 190 horsepower, the new powerplant was even smoother and quieter than the engine it replaced, improving still further Town Car silence and performance. At the same time, the Town Car's front suspension was reworked and four-wheel, anti-lock disc brakes were made standard. With the Continental, an electronic overdrive transaxle was made standard, while the Mark VII saw the Bill Blass Designer Series adopt most of the functional elements of the LSC edition.

The nation was hit with a major recession in 1991 and Lincoln sales suffered accordingly. The Town Car was down to 124,919, the Continental was down to 53,109, and the Mark VII fell to a miserable 9,299. The grand total—187,327 cars—still constituted the sixth best year in Lincoln history.

The recession continued to hold the nation in its grip in 1992, so it was probably just as well that there was very little to report in terms of new product developments at Lincoln. This was destined to be the final year for the Mark VII, so it was not surprising that there were few changes in that line. The grille texture was modestly revised and the lower bodyside molding on the LSC was changed to light gray. That was about it. Alterations were even less cosmic with the Continental where a revised hood ornament led the list. The Town Car, too, was continued essentially as before, the major development being that a passenger-side air bag became standard.

Lincoln sales were down only modestly despite the recession. A total of

160,012 cars of all types were built, including 113,458 Town Cars, 40,822 Continentals, and 5,732 Mark VIIs.

Although the all-new Mark VIII was the big push in 1993, there was news to report with other Lincoln lines, as well. The Town Car received its first freshening since the 1990 overhaul. New grille, tail lamps, and wheels were featured, in addition to a host of detail changes inside and out. Two interest-

1991 Town Car.

1991 Engine.

ing new options were a handling package and the integrated voice-activated cellular telephone shared with the Mark VIII. The Continental received similar detail refinements—including the optional cellular phone—but the big news was the five-passenger seating option. Designed to make the Continental more competitive with the international class of mid-size sedans, this option featured individual bucket seats and a center console.

Capturing the hearts of "youthful, influential and value-conscious professional" buyers was one of the design missions established for the Mark VIII, for those behind the project knew they were waging a demographic battle, as well. The average luxury car buyer was in his mid-1950s, and the strong appeal of the Town Car to this buyer segment had been the main engine that had powered Lincoln's sales advances in the 1980s and early 1990s. To continue to grow in the years and decades ahead, however, Lincoln had to find a way to appeal to a much younger buyer group—the luxury car buyers of the early 21st Century—without alienating Lincoln's existing customer base. To accomplish that, the design had to be both innovative and timeless. It would also need to pilot new technologies, features, and low-volume manufacturing processes.

Other than its radical new shape, the most dramatic element in the Mark

1992 Continental.

VIII was the new dual-overhead-cam (DOHC) Mark VIII powerplant. The two major changes from the original Lincoln 4.6-liter modular single-overhead-cam engine (SOHC) were the four-cam, 32-valve aluminum cylinder heads, and aluminum block construction. Bore and stroke dimensions were identical. The DOHC version of the engine delivered about 30 percent more power than the larger Ford 5-liter HO engine, and 33 percent more power than the 4.6 SOHC engine in its 210-horsepower dual-exhaust form.

The Mark VIII also broke new ground for Ford in terms of transmission technology with a completely new electronically controlled four-speed overdrive automatic transmission. A refinement of Ford's existing automatic transmission, it had a higher torque capacity and electronic control of more functions, for smoother shifting and greater fuel economy.

Mark VIII options included a power glass moonroof with a sliding privacy cover, an electrochromatic automatic-dimming inside/outside driver-side rearview mirror system, and a set of four brushed aluminum directional wheels. These wheels were also available in chrome.

The standard in-car entertainment system of the Mark VIII was an electronic AM/FM auto-reverse stereo cassette system combined with the Lincoln Premium Sound System. There were three in-car entertainment system options, starting with the Ford/JBL audio system. Debuting on the Mark VIII was new speaker technology, which made use of neodymium rare earth magnets for four woofers in the eight- speaker JBL system. A compact disc (CD) player was also available.

The Mark VIII coupe rode on a wheelbase of 113 inches and measured 206.9 inches in overall length. It was 74.6 inches wide, with a front tread measurement of 61.6 inches and a rear tread measurement of 60.2 inches. Overall height of the Mark VIII was 53.6 inches, with a cowl height of 37.2 inches. The windshield slope angle was 64.4 degrees, and the backlight angle an even "faster" 68.7 degrees. Curb weight was 3,752 pounds. The overall shape produced a drag coefficient of 0.33, a full 15 percent improvement over the Mark VII.

It looked pretty good on paper. In the real world, alas, the Mark VIII was a dud. It was estimated that as many as 50,000 cars would be built during the 1993 model run. The market as a whole was up more than 7 percent as the nation emerged from the 1991–92 recession, but only 32,370 Mark VIIIs were built—about a third fewer than projected.

In retrospect, it wasn't all that difficult to see why the Mark VIII was greeted with such a tepid reception. It was based on the Thunderbird/Cougar platform that had been introduced several years earlier, and those cars had been major disappointments from the first. They were much larger and heavier than the development program called for and heads rolled at Ford Motor

1992 Town Car.

Company because of their deficiencies. The Mark VIII had all those flaws and, in addition, had styling that did not prove popular with luxury car buyers. Many considered it unacceptably plain for a car with a base sticker price of $36,040. Many simply thought it far too large for a personal luxury car.

Still, it wasn't a bad year for the brand overall. Total Lincoln production rose 10 percent. In addition to Mark VIII production, this included 118,040 Town Cars and 26,798 Continentals.

There were only detail refinements in the 1994 models. A dual exhaust sys-

Top, 1993 Mark VIII interior; *bottom*, 1993 Mark VIII.

tem was made standard on the Town Car, as was solar tinted glass, while horsepower was increased. The Continental, which was due for a major redesign the following year, received some suspension changes and a new memory feature on the remote keyless entry that automatically adjusted the driver's seat to a pre-set position each time it was activated. The Mark VIII, which had been redesigned the year before, offered new chrome wheel options, and a memory feature for the seats and outside mirrors.

Lincoln's model year production rose slightly to 197,719 units. This included 117,448 Town Cars, 52,107 Continentals, and 28,164 Marks. There was also one notable change in personnel: Keith Magee replaced Lee Miskowski as general manager.

For 1995, the Continental was completely redesigned and represented Lincoln's most aggressive attempt yet to meet the demands of buyers in the international-type sedan segment. In virtually every objective respect, the new Continental met or exceeded the high standards previously set by cars in this segment, whether of American, European, or Japanese origin.

No less than eighteen systems, components, and technologies featured on the new Continental were submitted by Ford Motor Company to the United States Patent Office for patent consideration. Those include items that ranged from the prosaic (the console-mounted cupholder mechanism) to the positively space age (the control algorithms in the Vehicle Dynamics Module [VDM] for

1994 Continental.

the semi-active suspension system). The latter item said a lot about the overall approach Lincoln-Mercury Division took in developing the new car.

The 1995 Continental harkened back, in a sense, to the days of coachbuilt luxury cars where personalized transportation was the name of the game. The Continental did not, of course, allow a customer to individualize the body, but, rather—thanks to the onrush of technology—permitted him to personally tailor an amazing variety of accessory and mechanical components. With this system, the driver could design his car to match his unique driving style

Top, 1995 Continental interior; *bottom*, 1995 Continental.

by selecting from a wide choice of features heretofore dictated by the factory: from activating, deactivating, or modifying the performance of certain electronic accessories, to altering the "feel" of the steering by selecting from among three levels of power assist, and the stiffness of the suspension by selecting from among three levels of suspension damping—all with a flick of a switch on the instrument panel. In addition, each of the three steering levels automatically provided maximum assist during parking, to ease low-speed maneuvering, and at freeway speed, to give the driver greater road feel. This was achieved by means of a network of interactive onboard electronic control systems that were unique to the Continental.

The design team leader was Ted Finney, Ford Motor Company's design executive for luxury cars, and the resulting Continental "look" sought to combine the needs of state-of-the-art international styling with traditional Lincoln cues. The final design was subjected to rigorous scrutiny by potential buyers long before it went into production.

The 1995 Continental also broke new ground with respect to body engineering. Extensive computer-aided engineering techniques were employed to make the body and structure substantially stronger, stiffer, and quieter on the road. The steel unibody incorporated advanced manufacturing techniques in structural adhesives and a variety of new metalworking techniques. The hood, decklid, and front fenders were fiberglass-reinforced. Through the use of these

1996 Mark VIII.

1997 Town Car.

advanced technologies, the torsional stiffness of the body was increased by about 40 percent as compared to the 1994 Taurus-based model.

To reduce body weight, but without sacrificing any of the enhanced strength, the Continental's body was the most composite-intensive production car Ford Motor Company had ever built. Sheet-molding compound (SMC) body panels, which were lighter than steel panels, easier to tool, and highly dent-resistant, were used for the front fenders, hood, and rear decklid.

Making it all go was a new version of the 4.6-liter DOHC, 32-valve V8 engine first used in the Mark VIII. With the Continental, it was mated to a transaxle for front-wheel-drive application. All in all, the 1995 Continental was quite an engineering achievement and would doubtless have made Henry Leland proud. The only thing it couldn't do was lure paying customers into their neighborhood Lincoln-Mercury dealerships. It was modestly popular, but not by a long shot the grand slam Lincoln-Mercury management expected. Despite being almost certainly the finest car ever to wear a Lincoln nameplate, and for all its technological excellence, it was totally lacking in—for want of a better term—sex appeal. It's styling simply didn't set the hormones racing and too few people were inspired to want one. (One wonders who those potential buyers were who critiqued the car before it went into production.) Worse, at a base price of $40,750 it was both the smallest and most expensive car in the Lincoln stable.

The 1995 Town Car received its first major freshening since the current series was launched in 1990. Exterior changes included new headlights, grille, taillights, bumpers, and bodyside molding. Inside, an electronic steering switch selector allowed drivers to select the type of steering effort they preferred. The Signature and Cartier models featured steering wheel-mounted stereo and climate controls. The Mark VIII coupe received a new instrument panel, and a limited-edition LSC model was added.

By the mid-1990s, the traditional model year that began in October and ended in August or September was only a dim memory. There were new model launches all year round, so trade sources finally recognized that comparing model year production numbers had become a confused mess that really didn't tell much, anyway. For this reason, they switched to calendar year figures. So during calendar year 1995, 157,584 Lincolns of all types were built. This number included 99,291 Town Cars, along with 15,961 Mark VIIIs and 42,332 Continentals.

The following year, 1996, was Lincoln's Diamond Anniversary. A special "75th Diamond Anniversary Edition" Continental was offered. Also offered were an onboard global positioning satellite to pinpoint your location for roadside assistance, medical help, and law enforcement in an emergency. Run-flat Michelin tires were offered, too.

The Town Car series featured engine upgrades, new automatic climate controls, and real wood on the Cartier Edition instrument panel. In addition, the 1995 limited-edition Mark VIII LSC returned as a regular offering. The Mark series also listed a Touring Package and a 75th Diamond Anniversary model.

Despite a booming economy, calendar year production was down 8 percent. Softening Continental and Mark VIII sales were primarily responsible. A total of 145,035 Lincolns were built overall. The Town Car accounted for the lion's share as usual: 94,695 units. A total of 34,925 Continentals were built, and only 15,415 Mark VIIIs. Lincoln-Mercury also got a new general manager this year when James G. O'Connor moved into the big office. He arrived on the scene just in time to get involved in the development of Lincoln's second smash hit of the decade: the forthcoming Navigator sport-utility.

The following year was a holding action with major development in the wings for 1998. There were no significant changes in the 1997 Town Car, while those on the Continental were minor. The latter now featured a single-key system that locked the doors, glove box, and trunk with a turn of the wrist, plus all-speed traction control.

The most notable changes were made with the Mark VIII in an attempt to bolster its sagging sales—although even there the effort was relatively minor. Hood, grille, and interior were slightly redesigned. The Marks also featured high-intensity discharge front headlamps, cornering lamps, a neon rear applique, and puddle lamps.

Lincoln production for calendar year 1997 was up sharply, largely due to early model year production of the Navigator. A total of 179,445 Lincolns were built of which 32,963 were 1998 Navigators. Town Car (94,594) and Continental (34,421) production was virtually unchanged. The Mark VIII showed a small increase to 17,467 units.

Lincoln had a remarkable year in 1998 in both the good and the bad sense. Cadillac was caught utterly off guard with Lincoln's entry into the large, luxury

Top, 1998 Town Car interior; *bottom*, 1998 Town Car.

sport-utility market. The Town Car received its first major redesign since 1990 and sold well at first. The Continental got its first significant freshening since 1995 and continued to sell about the same, which was a disappointment. Finally, the Mark VIII pretty much stopped selling altogether and was discontinued. But best of all, Lincoln outproduced Cadillac for the first time in history.

The most important news was the Navigator, a large sport-utility based closely on the Ford Expedition. Sport-utilities as passenger car substitutes were roaring hot in 1998 and getting hotter all the time—and Lincoln had one and Cadillac didn't. The Navigator was powered by a 5.4-liter SOHC V8 engine rated at 230 horsepower. Speed-sensitive power steering and four-wheel anti-lock disc brakes were features, as well as a load-leveling air suspension system. Body-on-frame construction gave it a tow weight of 8,000 lbs. It was available in both two- and four-wheel-drive models, and carried a base price of $43,300.

The 1998 Continental received a slew of styling changes intended to render it more visually appealing than the unexciting 1995–97 models. On the exterior, these consisted of a new grille, wraparound headlights, and bulging fenders. A new hood flowed into a windshield that was more steeply raked than before. The Continental's trunk was slightly longer and the massive tail lights were new. Inside, the passenger space was roomier and an entirely new instrument panel featured bird's-eye maple wood trim. The rear compartment featured a new folding center armrest with integrated cupholders.

1999 Mark VII.

The Mark VIII was unchanged from 1997, and it was announced in January that production would be discontinued in June. The Thunderbird platform, upon which the Mark VIII was based, had been discontinued in 1997. A few of the Mark VIII produced in 1998 were Collector's Editions, a special commemorative version announced in February. Based on the LSC model, the Collector's Edition was available in Cordovan or White Pearlescent. A wood-trimmed steering wheel and shift selector knob, and unique Collector's

Top, 1999 Town Car; *bottom*, 1998 Navigator.

Edition floor mats were also included in the package, as was special exterior badging. The most intriguing feature was the commemorative gift sent to each buyer: a set of numbered silver ingots representing the eight classic Mark designs in a black leather case. An additional ingot engraved with the vehicle's identification number was included with a certificate of authenticity signed by Jim O'Connor, Lincoln-Mercury's general manager. The base price for the Collector's Edition was $40,890.

Calendar year production reached an all-time record with 200,454 units accounted for. This included 47,305 Navigators and 153,140 cars. The breakdown was: Town Car, 110,718; Continental, 36,328; and Mark VIII, 6,103. In contrast, Cadillac built only 181,699 vehicles (5,521 of which were Escalade sport-utilites that had been rushed into production at the tail end of the year), so it was a solid and very satisfying win for Lincoln. If anyone in Dearborn noticed that Cadillac still sold 15 percent more cars than Lincoln, they weren't saying so. At any rate, that would change in 1999.

Lincoln-Mercury had a new boss in 1998, as well. In May, Mark Hutchins was named general manager, succeeding Jim O'Connor who moved over to Ford Division.

After the daunting exertions made in 1998, there was little news with the 1999 models. The biggest change for the brand involved personnel. In August, Gerry McGovern was appointed director of the Lincoln design studio. Previously, he had been director of Land Rover design. The move promised a European approach to future Lincoln styling.

As for the 1999 models, the Town Car received standard side airbags and a new JBL audio system. The Continental was similarly upgraded and also announced five new exterior colors, upgraded interior trim options, and two new wheel designs. In its second year, the Navigator offered more power, adjustable pedals, speed-sensitive stereo volume, and a hands-free cellular phone option.

Calendar year production declined slightly from 1998's sizzling pace. A total of 190,633 vehicles were built, including 42,690 trucks and 147,944 cars. Still, Lincoln outproduced Cadillac in both categories this time, although the lead in cars was only a couple thousand units. The breakdown in Lincoln passenger car production for the calendar year (which included early LS units that were officially 2000 models) was: Town Car, 81,551; LS, 39,266; and Continental, 27,121.

It had been a fantastic decade. Starting with the highly successful launch of the new Town Car in 1990, the brand had been catapulted into the lead in production and sales among American luxury manufacturers. It was unfortunate that Lincoln's position was thrown into turmoil at just that time . . .

CHAPTER ELEVEN

2003 Lincoln Town Car BPS.

Lincoln Looks to the Future: 2000–Up

LINCOLN ENTERED the new millennium in the best shape it had ever known. It had vanquished arch rival Cadillac two years in a row and, even if it didn't last, rough parity had been achieved. The LS, which was launched in the spring of 1999 as a 2000 model, was off to a hot start, and Lincoln's sport-utility continued to draw in the customers.

Yet, there were storm clouds on the horizon. Cadillac had introduced a completely restyled DeVille line for 2000 that found favor with luxury car buyers. In addition, the ramping up of production of Cadillac's Escalade sport-utility tightened the sales race significantly.

By mid-2000, Lincoln had managed to hold onto its place as the leading luxury vehicle in the United States, but industry analysts were predicting it would be the last time an American brand would take the title in the foreseeable future. They cited surging sales of European and Japanese luxury brands such as BMW, Mercedes-Benz, and Lexus. So Lincoln had won its seventy-eight-year-old battle with Cadillac only to find the rules of the game had changed.

As recently as 1990, Lincoln and Cadillac had dominated American sales for luxury vehicles. Then the Baby-Boomers arrived, to be followed—eventually—by the Gen Xers who in time would become the customer base for luxury vehicles. Those groups, the experts were finding, preferred the sporty-handling of a BMW, or the styling and quality of a Mercedes or a Lexus over traditional American concepts of automotive luxury.

Then Lincoln got caught up in corporate politics.

In February, 2000, it was announced that Ford would relocate the American headquarters of all its luxury brands to Irvine, California, and fold them all into a new Premier Automotive Group (PAG). This would include not only Lincoln, but also Jaguar, Volvo, Aston Martin and Land Rover. Throughout the 1990s, Ford had been on a buying binge and mostly what it bought were luxury brands. So now Lincoln found itself in competition not only with the likes of BMW, Mercedes-Benz, and Lexus on the outside, but other brands within the company itself. Lincoln fielded models in competition with all the recently acquired Ford luxury brands except Aston Martin. Worse, Ford was spending billions to turn Jaguar into a full-line volume competitor.

What Lincoln's place would be in the new order of things was anybody's guess. Certainly no one at the Premier Automotive Group offered much help. In ensuing months, statements appeared from time to time saying that Lincoln's mission was under discussion or that Lincoln's mission would be to build "American-style luxury" or vague things like that. But wasn't it precisely traditional American-style luxury that was on the way out—even with American buyers?[1] The problem was put into focus with an analysis of the Lincoln LS. The company described the LS this way:

> Defying the rules of 'old luxury,' the 2001 Lincoln LS makes a bold statement of American luxury, combining style, power and spirited performance in a premium automotive package.[2]

The LS did indeed have a contemporary look to it, without some of the stylistic excesses that marred Lincolns in the past. Up front, the trademark Lincoln waterfall grille was nicely done, and the heavy chrome surround at the back, which housed the back-up lights and the license plate, was handsome. This latter design cue was also becoming a Lincoln trademark.

In fact, the LS was a good-looking car from any exterior angle and made for an interesting comparison with the S-Type. The late Jeff Lawson, who was chief designer on the Jag, once said that the only part of that design with which he was less than completely satisfied was the rear end.[3] Presumably, he was referring to the somewhat stubby appearance when viewed from certain angles. Even though the LS shared the same basic body and proportions with the S-Type, Lincoln designers managed to avoid this shortcoming.

2000 LS.

The LS interior was less successful. The S-Type's interior design was simply beautiful and reeked of what Lawson liked to call "Jaguar DNA." In contrast, the interior of the LS was oddly sterile. All the right pieces were there (many of them shared with the S-Type), but they made no statement. Many automotive journalists thought the LS looked downright plain inside.

The standard engine was a 210 horsepower, 3.0-liter, DOHC V6. It could be combined with a Getrag five-speed manual transmission or with the Select-Shift automatic. There was also an optional 3.9-liter V8 of this engine that pumped out 252 horsepower and used a true dual exhaust system for optimum engine performance.

So far so good, if the LS was taken on its own merits. The problem came with a comparison between the LS and the S-Type. Sharing platforms with Jaguar was fine in theory, but if Lincoln was going to be constrained from the get-go to being sort of a not-quite-as-good Jaguar what did that say about Lincoln's future within the Ford stable? It was a good question, but no answer was forthcoming from the halls of the Premier Automotive Group.

The LS was introduced in 1999 as a 2000 model. For 2001, Lincoln offered several of what it called "enhancements" to the line. These consisted of all-speed traction control standard on the V6 manual, a glow-in-the-dark manual trunk release, rear-seat lower child-safety seat tether anchors, and additional power point added to the rear of the front center console, a compass included in the electrochromic interior rearview mirror (optional on V6 mod-

Premier Automotive Group vehicles at Pebble Beach in 2001.

els), four new exterior colors, and optional 17-inch chrome wheels with the Sport Package

The Town Car had a new model for 2001: the Town Car Cartier L, which Lincoln Mercury Division—they weren't using the hyphen anymore—called the "ultimate Town Car" It was a factory-produced long-wheelbase which model extended six inches to provide an additional 7.5 cubic feet of space for rear seat passengers. Said Lincoln President Mark Hutchins (the general manager was now president of Lincoln Mercury):

> The Town Car Cartier L is designed for consumers who want an even roomier, more luxurious, full-size sedan with all the comforts and amenities Lincoln customers expect in a luxury automobile. Town Car Cartier L adds to Lincoln's history of providing consumers with luxury motoring to meet their every need. Arriving in a Town Car always has meant something special, and we intend to keep it that way.

Other features offered with the Cartier L included wider rear-door openings, rear heated seats, a folding armrest with storage bins, rear audio and climate controls, redundant seat controls, mood lighting and a cigar-size ashtray with illuminated lighter.

One reason for the creation of the Cartier L was Lincoln's leadership position in the livery market where it held a commanding 85 percent market share. Cadillac was the owner of most of the other 15 percent. A similar version made exclusively for fleet and livery dealers—called Executive L—shared most features with the Cartier L.

In another move to solidify its rear against an insurgent Cadillac, Lincoln decided to compete with GM's popular and profitable OnStar system. Some 2001 Lincoln models featured a mobile phone that linked drivers to the company's Rescu system, which offered features similar to those of OnStar. Lincoln's phones operated on the Sprint PCS network and, unlike the GM hardware, was capable of being removed from the vehicle and used separately. The Lincoln/Sprint system also offered limited Internet access.

There were other changes and features on the 2001 Lincoln range. The Town Car offered a more powerful engine, advanced restraint system air bags, seat belt pretensioners, and power adjustable pedals. The Continental added a standard universal garage door opener. The Navigator offered an auxiliary climate control system. In addition, Lincoln's Complimentary Maintenance program, announced in May for all 2001-model Lincolns, was a first for an American luxury brand. The program covered all routine maintenance, from oil changes to wipers to shocks, for the first three years or 36,000 miles. The basic Lincoln warranty of four years/50,000 miles remained in place.

A typically equipped Navigator 4x2 was priced at $46,360 that year, or $270 (0.6 percent) more than the 2000 model. A typically equipped 2001 Lincoln Town Car Signature series was $42,640, up $485 (1.2 percent) over the 2000 model.

Then there was the curious saga of the Lincoln Blackwood. It was previewed at the auto shows in 1999 as a Navigator with a pickup bed in back where the Navigator's rear cargo area used to be—a combination sport-utility and pickup truck. Lincoln promised to build it as an "auto show concept vehicle brought to life."[4] It said the Blackwood would be available at Lincoln dealerships in the first half of 2001 and would be built in Claycomo, Missouri, near Kansas City, with production limited to fewer than 10,000 per year. As it turned out, the number was far fewer even than that. The Blackwood did, indeed, appear in 2001 carrying a sticker price of over $50,000. After a few months on sale, it was withdrawn from production and nothing was ever heard about it again. It wasn't based on the Navigator, either. When the Blackwood did appear—however briefly—it was based on the much smaller Ford Explorer platform. But all was not lost, for many of the bits and pieces reappeared a year later on the Explorer-based 2003 Lincoln Aviator sport-utility.

2000 Town Car.

During its short life, the Blackwood featured a four passenger cabin trimmed in black leather and real wood. The exterior featured a distinctive box-like trunk with a power-operated tonneau cover. The exotic, heavily striated African Wenge wood of the show vehicle was interpreted for production in a three-dimensional composite surface for better durability, maintenance, and insurability than wood. The interior of the trunk was trimmed with brushed stainless steel and accented with LED light strips. The only optional feature was a console-integrated, satellite-based navigation system.

The Blackwood's 5.4-liter, V8 engine produced 300 horsepower. It was mated to a four-speed automatic transmission with overdrive and a locking torque converter. A 3.73 final drive ratio and a built-in Class III/IV hitch contributed to a tow rating of 8,700 pounds.

Easy come, easy go.

The major product news for 2002 was the Continental Collector's Edition. Continental sales had plummeted following the introduction of the LS and the division had decided to discontinue it. As with the Mark VIII in its final months, a special edition was offered.

Approximately 2,000 Collector's Editions were planned for production and the model included the following key features: genuine walnut burl steering wheel, instrument panel and side door trim with the "CE" logo, "preferred suede" seat inserts with "milled pebble" leather bolsters, ten-spoke chrome wheels, a platinum painted grille, and the CE logo on exterior bodyside and inscribed on the floormats. The Continental Collector's Edition was offered at $41,120.

There was also a modest freshening of the Town Car in 2002, mostly involving a wider, bolder waterfall grille. The big story in 2002, however, was the 2003 Lincoln Aviator, which went into production in the summer of 2002 and is going on sale as this book is written. The Aviator is an Explorer-based sport-utility vehicle built on a 113.7-inch wheelbase. It has an advanced dual overhead cam, four-valve V8 engine, a sophisticated four-wheel independent suspension and is available with all-wheel drive. The Aviator will have flexible seating for up to seven people and carries a base price of $39,995. Said Darryl Hazel, who had been named president of Lincoln Mercury Division in the latter part of 2001:

> Aviator brings Lincoln-luxury to the extremely popular and competitive mid-sized SUV segment. Think of Aviator as a seven-eighths scale Navigator, and you get an idea of the design. Think of Aviator as a Lincoln, and you get an idea of the level of luxury and value this vehicle brings to the market.[5]

The New York International Auto Show in April, 2003, saw two interesting Lincoln products—one a concept and the other a limited production model. Lincoln sought to give its luxury SUV a boost by unveiling the Navigator K concept. With a 385 horsepower from a supercharged 5.4-liter V8 engine, the Navigator K is the first Lincoln concept vehicle from the Ford Performance Group.

A new armored Lincoln Town Car Ballistic Protection Series also made its public debut at the New York show. Scheduled for production in mid-2003, the Lincoln Town Car BPS was designed to provide a high level of armored protection, with high quality, at a competitive price. The times in which we live . . .

Lincoln Mercury's concern about Lincoln's plan in the grand scheme of things had led to action in the spring of 2001. The result was the MK 9 show car, which stands as the most intriguing suggestion as to the future direction

2000 Town Car.

of the brand. Lincoln Design Director Gerry McGovern had been assigned to get Lincoln out of a demographic bind. McGovern liked to point out that the average age of buyers of the Town Car was seventy-one years old, and that the company had best get its act together before its customer base died off.[6] Jetting between Dearborn and his home in England near Coventry, McGovern was working on giving Lincoln vehicles a look that would unite all models the company produced. Most radical of all, McGovern said the new designs would be determined by his tastes or that of the designers working under him, as opposed to the design-by-focus-group approach that has become the norm in the industry.

The Lincoln MK 9 coupe concept points to the design direction of future Lincoln vehicles and is a statement of the brand's "American Luxury" signature. The concept—unveiled at the 2001 New York Auto Show—featured "optimized proportions and stance, combined with an overall restraint in execution."[7] The interior was designed to be "indulgent and comfortable—all characteristics that define 'American Luxury.'" Said McGovern:

> The Lincoln MK 9 displays a timeless elegance borne of the design's inherent simplicity and visual logic, while its overall exuberance is unmistakably American. During the next several years, Lincoln will build on the design direction evident in the MK 9 through new concept and production vehicles.
>
> Lincoln has given me an incredible opportunity to hand-select a team of the best young designers from all over the world to explore the brand's heritage and build a design philosophy around the tangible and emotional qualities that define America and American Luxury.
>
> We have a holistic view of product design that is different from a traditional automotive approach. Lincoln Design and our show properties like the MK 9 are about defining and embracing a philosophy to guide every step of the product development process.[8]

Traditional Lincoln and Continental features obvious on the MK 9's exterior start with the chrome-accented upper beltline that runs the length of the vehicle. Gloss black paint highlights the body surfaces. The face of the MK 9 incorporates an evolution of a Lincoln signature grille flanked by twin xenon gas discharge headlamps, with turn signal indicators integrated into each lamp unit.

The front fenders include functional air vents. Each fender outlet is part of a ring frame that traces the sill and door aperture to enhance structural integrity. The ring frames also act as mounting surfaces for the machined aluminum door hinges, which provide articulation to improve ingress and egress. The lower sections of the ring frames are exposed to give highlights along the rocker surfaces. The aluminum door handles are flush-mounted to the door skin and are operated by remote control.

The enormous 22-inch, 10-spoke aluminum alloy wheels are fitted with P275/45/R22 Continental tires in front and P295/40/R22 tires in the rear. Twin rectangular dual exhaust outlets are framed by the rear bumper fascia, and compliment the horizontal emphasis of the red LED tail lamps.

Inside, a combination of Dark Cherry Red and Marlboro Red leathers with accents of polished metal creates a luxurious lounge environment. Dark

Top, 2002 LS Sport; *bottom*, 2002 Blackwood.

Cherry saddle leather is used for the flooring, and white leather is used for the headliner. The front seats—which are cantilevered off the center console to improve passenger foot space—take their design influence from the Eames Lounge Chair, a mid-20th Century American classic, which was designed for comfort. Moreover, there are visual connections between exterior and interior, such as the body-colored seat shells and the horizontal chrome finishers. The symmetrical dashboard is clean and simple with etched glass instruments re-crafted with jewel-like quality and illuminated indirectly.

The MK 9's controls are a combination of advanced digital and analog interfaces. Navigation and telematics information is displayed on a reconfigurable screen in the center console that is operated by retractable controls that sit flush when not in use. The transmission selection is by an electronic, column-mounted paddle shifter. The center and roof consoles have dimmable electro-luminescent light panels behind translucent metallic surfaces. Individual spotlights mounted in the headliner use fiber-optic technology. Said Mark Hutchins, then-president of Lincoln Mercury:

> The Lincoln MK 9 is the first tangible expression of the new values and philosophy that will guide Lincoln's growth in North America, and eventually, in Europe and other markets around the world.
>
> Lincoln's goals for the new decade are simple, but challenging: build on our strengths in North America, grow the business and achieve global desirability. Regardless of which markets the vehicles are sold in or when, Lincolns should be recognized for timeless design, indulgent comfort and effortless performance. But as they evolve, Lincolns always will be distinctively and unabashedly American.[9]

The company saw the MK 9 as a logical extension of trends already in place. The Town Car and other traditional Lincolns, it decided, primarily appealed to affluent consumers who favored large, conservatively styled vehicles. But the Lincoln Navigator sport-utility, introduced in 1998, and the Lincoln LS, introduced for 2000, attracted a new customer base. Sixty percent of Navigator customers and nearly 70 percent of LS customers had never owned a Lincoln before. Furthermore, the median customer age for both the Navigator and the LS was in the early fifties, compared with well over sixty for the Town Car. Said McGovern:

> The consumers driving the luxury market today—and the future customers building their careers now—are very design-aware.

As evidence of the growing appetite of Americans and Europeans for design, McGovern points to the success of products such as Apple's notebook computers, Zero Halliburton cases (which are both American products) and the popularity of designer hotels, such as Avalon Hotel in Beverly Hills. He continued:

> It is appropriate for Lincoln, as an American brand, to claim automotive design leadership because Americans have always been very receptive to innovative design. The freedom of expression in America, and the youthful character and optimistic nature of Americans has produced truly influential designers and architects such as Charles Eames and Pierre Koenig. For the same reasons, America has always had great appeal to innovators from all over the world. People such as Ludwig Mies van der Rohe, Le Corbusier and Eero Saarinen did some of their best work here.[10]

According to McGovern, the Lincoln design team, which includes interior designers, modelers, materials experts and packaging engineers, began their work by exploring Lincoln's heritage. He noted:

> Before we could define what Lincoln design should stand for in the future, we first had to understand its past. In our exploration, we learned that two Lincoln coupes—the 1940 Continental and the 1956 Continental Mark II—

2003 Aviator Kitty Hawk Edition.

followed by the iconic Continental sedans and convertibles of the 1960s, had tremendous cache and were incredible design statements. Interestingly, they all have design elements that are still appropriate in a modern context.

McGovern said the 1940 Continental—a car that architect Frank Lloyd Wright declared to be the most beautiful car in the world—was significant for its sheer elegance. The Continental, which was commissioned by Edsel Ford and designed by E.T. Gregorie, was the first vehicle honored for design excellence by the Museum of Modern Art in New York.

The Mark II, designed and built under the direction of William Clay Ford, Sr., was envisioned as the contemporary evolution of the original Continental. The Mark II established the classic hood, cabin and deck proportions of the modern luxury coupe and was an oasis of restraint in a market dominated by tail fins, chrome and exaggerated styling elements.

The 1961 Continental, designed by Elwood Engel, remains one of the most enduring automotive designs of all time. Its sheer body surfaces, unique center-opening doors, chrome-accented shoulder line and overall restraint established a signature look for Lincoln that was unique. Pablo Picasso owned a Continental from this era. They still have tremendous visual impact and have been featured in several popular films, including "The Matrix." Said McGovern:

> When a brand has such a strong design heritage as Lincoln, the challenge is to recognize the past without being held back by it. Between the 1940s and the 1960s, Lincolns were about beautiful proportions, elegant sophistication and restraint. These are qualities we can realize in a modern context without being at all retrospective.
>
> In our exploration, we asked ourselves what creates luxury and what gives great designs their longevity. Then we looked at the qualities of various pieces of design to help communicate our idea of American Luxury.
>
> Often, when people think of contemporary architecture or modern furniture design, they think of something cold and austere. We will deliver designs that are contemporary, but also warm, inviting, indulgent and highly functional.

Continuity and consistency also are important elements for Lincoln, according to McGovern:

> "There are luxury brands that essentially build small, medium and large versions of the same product. This will not be our approach. Our vehicles will have a high level of differentiation while being bound together by a common design DNA."

Exposed engineering is another feature the Lincoln team finds desirable, as exemplified by the Meda office chair, designed by Alberto Meda. McGovern added:

> Much of the structure and mechanisms of the Meda chair are left exposed because they are beautiful. We are going to strive for the same level of execution in Lincoln vehicles. A hinge or a seat bracket must serve a function,

MK 9 show car.

> but there is no reason why they cannot be both functional and beautiful. The most sophisticated premium products have great precision, tactility and logic in their controls.
>
> Luxury is not something that can be applied—it must be intrinsic. A car's surfaces, its jewelry and materials—whether they are metal, wood, leather, plastic or fabric—must be appropriate to their job, beautifully rendered and expertly crafted.

During the next several years, Lincoln intends to enter new market segments while continuing to refine the luxury and performance of its current portfolio of vehicles. The evolution of today's vehicles and the introduction of the next generation of Lincolns that fully reflect the new design philosophy will be led by a partnership of design, engineering, purchasing and manufacturing.

It may actually work out that way. At least Lincoln is back home in Detroit. As this book was being readied, Ford Motor Company announced that Lincoln Mercury would abandon Irvine, California, and return to Dearborn in the summer of 2003.

Maybe there's hope after all.

Notes

CHAPTER ONE, 1946–48

The most important resources drawn upon in the writing of this chapter include Allan Nevins' *Ford: Decline and Rebirth, 1933–1962* and the author's interview with E. T. Gregorie. Ford Motor Company papers in the author's collection also supplied significant material.

CHAPTER TWO, 1949–51

The most important resources drawn upon in the writing of this chapter include Allan Nevins' *Ford: Decline and Rebirth, 1933–1962* and the author's interview with E. T. Gregorie. Ford Motor Company papers in the author's collection also supplied significant material.

1. Ford Motor Company papers, author's collection.
2. The parade car was revised in 1954 at the behest of President Dwight D. Eisenhower. He objected to using the convertible top during inclement weather because it blocked him from the view of the people, so Ford Motor Company arranged to have a removable Plexiglas top constructed for the rear compartment. Following this modification, the car was invariably referred to as the "bubbletop." It was retired as the primary presidential parade car in the early months of 1961, but remained on duty as a back-up vehicle at least through 1965.
3. Ford Motor Company papers, author's collection.

CHAPTER THREE, 1952–55

The most important resources drawn upon in the writing of this chapter include Allan Nevins' *Ford: Decline and Rebirth, 1933–1962* and various issues of *Motor Trend* magazine. Ford Motor Company papers in the author's collection also supplied significant material.

1. Woudenberg, p. 47.
2. This raises all sorts of questions regarding the development process of the overhead-valve engine. One thing engineers normally check to determine if different en-

gines are from the same engine family is the bore centers. The fact that the camshafts interchanged would mean that the two engines shared the same bore centers and the interchangeability of the lifters would add further evidence. While the two engines had nothing else obviously in common, it is possible that Lincoln engineers, in their rush to get the overhead-valve engine to market, started by attempting to convert the 1949-series L-head to overhead valves. It wouldn't have been the only time this had been tried. In later years, American Motors did it with its inline six.

3. Ford Motor Company papers, author's collection.

CHAPTER FOUR, 1956–57

The most important resources drawn upon in the writing of this chapter include the author's interview with Richard Stout, Allan Nevins' *Ford: Decline and Rebirth, 1933–1962* and various issues of *Motor Trend* magazine. Ford Motor Company papers in the author's collection also supplied significant material.

1. See *Disaster In Dearborn: The Edsel Story*, Stanford University Press.
2. Woudenberg, p. 66.
3. *Motor Trend*, Nov., 1955, p. 65.
4. It is fascinating how standards have changed. When the author first started writing about Lincoln in 1980, this was still the view of "quality" manufacturing technique. Within a few years, though, it came to be realized that all those inspectors were merely covering (if unwittingly) for inefficiencies in the manufacturing process and that the quality solution was to get to the root of the problem so that parts were made right to begin with and, thus, render inspections superfluous.
5. *Motor Trend*, Nov., 1955, p. 65.
6. Ibid, p. 36.
7. A few Eldorado Broughams were built as 1959 and 1960 models, but the bodies were farmed out to Ghia in Italy. Production of this second series Brougham amounted to exactly 200 units for both model years combined.

CHAPTER FIVE, 1958–60

The most important resources drawn upon in the writing of this chapter include the author's interview with Richard Stout, Allan Nevins' *Ford: Decline and Rebirth, 1933–1962* and various issues of *Motor Trend* magazine. Ford Motor Company papers in the author's collection also supplied significant material.

1. *Motor Trend*, Dec., 1957.
2. Actually, over a two year period beginning in 1957, Continental Division was merged into Lincoln Division, then Lincoln was merged with Mercury to form Lincoln and Mercury Division (no hyphens), then Edsel was merged into Lincoln and Mercury to form the Mercury-Edsel-Lincoln Division. A year-and-a-half later, the Edsel brand was discontinued and it became Lincoln-Mercury Division once again. It remained so until 1999 when the hyphen was deleted making it Lincoln Mercury Division, which it remains as this is written.

CHAPTER SIX, 1961–65

The most important resource drawn upon in the writing of this chapter includes Ford Motor Company papers in the author's collection.

1. Engel interview, author's collection.
2. *Car Life*, March, 1961, p. 17.
3. *Car Life*, March, 1961, p. 11.
4. Modifications included numerous mechanical changes: a special; high performance Lincoln V8 engine; heavy-duty transmission; heavy-duty suspension; heavy-duty steering; heavy-duty brakes; heavy-duty axle; and special tires. The bubbletop was made a permanent bulletproof glass structure, with a detachable black cover that could be used when privacy was desired. The agent grip handles at the back were permanently fixed in an extended position atop the deck lid, and an extra retractable step plate was added just ahead of each rear wheel. As far as cosmetics were concerned, the interior trim patterns were updated and the car was fitted with what appears to have been a 1962 grille. Still later, 1965 tail light lenses were added.
5. Ford Motor Company papers, author's collection.
6. *Motor Trend*, July, 1963, p. 41.

CHAPTER SEVEN, 1966–69

The most important resource drawn upon in the writing of this chapter includes Ford Motor Company papers in the author's collection.

1. Pronounced "low."
2. Ford Motor Company papers, author's collection.
3. One has to wonder why Ford stylists didn't simply attempt a modern evocation of the distinctive and beautiful radiator used by classic-era Lincolns, such as the magnificent 1932 KB-Series.
4. *Car Life*, March, 1968, p. 75
5. *Motor Trend*, April, 1968.

CHAPTER EIGHT, 1970-76

The most important resources drawn upon in the writing of this chapter include the author's interview with David Holls. Ford Motor Company papers in the author's collection also supplied significant material.

1. *Motor Trend*, Aug., 1969, p. 97.

CHAPTER NINE, 1977–84

The most important resource drawn upon in the writing of this chapter includes Ford Motor Company papers in the author's collection.

1. The whole point of the Williamsburg option had been simplicity, but Lincoln designers just couldn't help themselves.
2. Ford Motor Company papers, author's collection.
3. *Motor Trend*, Aug., 1979, pp. 75–79.
4. *Car and Driver*, Sept., 1979, p. 43.
5. *Motor Trend*, Feb., 1982, p. 67.
6. *Motor Trend*, Aug., 1983, pp. 28-29.
7. *Car and Driver*, Aug., 1983, p. 55.

CHAPTER TEN, 1985–99

The most important resources drawn upon in the writing of this chapter include interviews with Robert Rewey, Ross Roberts and Lee Miskowski. Ford Motor Company papers in the author's collection also supplied significant material.

1. *Motor Trend*, Oct., 1987, p. 62.
2. *Palm Beach Illustrated*, No. 1, 1989, p. 42.
3. George H. W. Bush was the forty-first president. His son, George W. Bush, is the forty-third.
4. *Palm Springs Life*, Nov., 1989, p. 229.

CHAPTER ELEVEN, 2000–UP

The most important resource drawn upon in the writing of this chapter includes Ford Motor Company papers in the author's collection.

1. Don't even ask about the role of the Mercury. When Lincoln-Mercury moved to California and Lincoln was swallowed up by the Premier Automotive Group, the Mercury brand was essentially turned loose into a limbo with no one responsible for it. Ford officials were then shocked—genuinely shocked!—when this situation prompted an unending stream of questions from the press corps regarding the future (if any) of the Mercury brand . . .
2. Ford Motor Company papers, author's collection.
3. Lawson interview, author's collection.
4. Ford Motor Company papers, author's collection.
5. Ford Motor Company papers, author's collection.
6. Of course, people have been saying the same thing since Henry Leland was in the business. Buyers of luxury brands are always old for the simple reason that old people are the ones who like luxury most and have the most money to pay for it.
7. Ford Motor Company papers, author's collection.
8. McGovern interview, Ford Motor Company papers, author's collection.
9. Ford Motor Company papers, author's collection.
10. McGovern interview, Ford Motor Company papers, author's collection.

Bibliography

PRIMARY SOURCES

Books

Bennett, Harry. *We Never Called Him Henry.* New York, 1951.
Chrysler Corporation. Annual Reports, brochures and miscellaneous publications. Highland Park, Michigan.
Detroit Public Library, Automotive History Collection.
Ford Archives, Henry Ford Museum
Ford Motor Company. Annual Reports, brochures and miscellaneous publications. Detroit, Michigan.
General Motors Corporation. Annual Reports, brochures and miscellaneous publications. Detroit, Michigan.
Hudson Motor Car Company. Annual Reports, brochures and miscellaneous publications. Detroit, Michigan.
Packard Motor Car Company. Annual Reports, brochures and miscellaneous publications. Detroit, Michigan.
Pfau, Hugo. *The Custom Body Era.* New York, 1970.
Sloan, Alfred P. *Adventures of a White-Collar Man.* New York, 1941.
Sloan, Alfred P., Jr. *My Years With General Motors.* Garden City, New York, 1964.
Sorensen, Charles E. *My Forty Years With Ford.* New York, 1956.
Stout, Richard H. *Make 'Em Shout Hooray!* New York, 1988.
Studebaker Corporation (Delaware). Annual Reports, brochures and miscellaneous publications. South Bend, Indiana.
Studebaker-Packard Corporation. Annual Reports, brochures and miscellaneous publications. Detroit, Michigan, and South Bend, Indiana.
Studebaker-Packard Papers, George Arents Research Library, Syracuse University. Syracuse, New York.
Studebaker-Worthington Corporation. Annual Reports and miscellaneous publications. New York, New York.
Western Reserve Historical Society, Cleveland, Ohio.

Interviews

By the author with John Conde, Charles Jordan, Mark Gjovic, E. T. "Bob" Gregorie, David Holls, Semon E. Knudsen, Holden Koto, Lee Miskowski, Robert Rewey, Ross Roberts, Richard Stout, Richard Teague, and Rich Thomas.

Periodicals

Action Era Vehicle, Advertising Age, American Way, Argosy, Autocar (G.B.), *Auto Age, Automobile Quarterly, Automobile Show, Automobile, Automotive Industries, Automotive News, Automobile Topics, AutoWeek, Boston Globe, Business Week, Car Classics, Car Craft, Car & Driver, Car Life, CARS, Cars & Parts, Consumer Reports, Detroit News, Esquire, Forbes, Fortune, Handbook of Gasoline Automobiles, Horseless Age, Motor* (G.B.), *Hot Rod, Industrial Design, Mechanix Illustrated, Motor* (U.S.), *Motor Age, Motor Life, Motor Trend, Motor Trend Yearbook* (1955–61), *N.A.D.A. Used Car Guide* (various issues, 1934–67), *Newsweek, New York Times, Popular Mechanics, Popular Science, Road & Track, Scientific American, Special-Interest Autos, Sports Car Graphic, Time, True's Automobile Yearbook* (1953–60), *Wall Street Journal, Ward's,* and *Washington Post.*

SECONDARY SOURCES

Allen, Frederick Lewis. *The Big Change: America Transforms Itself, 1900–1950.* New York, 1952.
Barker, Ronald and Anthony Harding. *Automobile Design: Great Designers and Their Work.* Cambridge, Massachussetts, 1970.
Beasely, Norman and George W. Stark. *Made in Detroit.* New York, 1957.
Boyd, T. A. *Professional Amateur.* New York, 1957.
Brierly, Brooks T. *Auburn, Reo, Franklin and Pierce-Arrow versus Cadillac, Chrysler, Lincoln and Packard.* Coconut Grove, Florida, 1991.
Brinkley, David. *Washington Goes to War.* New York, 1988.
Bury, Martin H. *The Automobile Dealer.* Philadelphia, 1958.
Catton, Bruce. *The War Lords of Washington.* New York, 1948.
Chandler, Alfred D., Jr. *Giant Enterprise.* New York, 1964.
Cohn, David L. *Combustion On Wheels.* Boston, 1944.
Colins, Herbert Ridgeway. *Presidents On Wheels.* New York, 1971.
Conde, John. *American Motors Family Album.* Detroit, 1969.
Cornell Auto Publications. *Automobile Value Review.* Chicago, 1941.
Crabb, Richard. *Birth of a Giant.* New York, 1969.
Cravens, J. K. *Automobile Year Book and Buyer's Guide Illustrated.* Chicago, 1934.
Cravens, J. K. *Automobile Year Book and Buyer's Guide Illustrated.* Chicago, 1937.
Cray, Ed, *Chrome Colossus.* New York, 1980.
Drucker, Peter F. *Concept of the Corporation.* New York, 1946.
Drucker, Peter F. *The Practice of Management.* New York, 1954.
Editors of Automobile Quarterly. *The American Car Since 1775.* New York, 1971.
Georgano, G. N., ed. *The Complete Encyclopedia of Commercial Vehicles.* Osceola, Wisconsin, 1979.
Georgano, G. N., ed. *The Complete Encyclopedia of Motorcars: 1885 to the Present.* New York, 1973.

Gustin, Lawrence R. *Billy Durant, Creator of General Motors.* Grand Rapids, Michigan, 1973.

Heasley, Jerry. *The Production Figure Book for U.S. Cars.* Osceola, Wisconsin, 1977.

Hendry, Maurice. *Cadillac: The Standard of the World.* Princeton, New Jersey, 1973.

Herndon, Booton. *Ford.* New York, 1969.

Iacocca, Lido A. *Iacocca, An Autobiography.* New York, 1984.

Keats, John. *Insolent Chariots.* Philadelphia, 1958.

Kimes, Beverly R., ed. *Packard: A History of the Motorcar and the Company.* Princeton, New Jersey, 1978.

Kimes, Beverly Rae, and Henry Austin Clark, Jr. *Standard Catalog of American Cars 1805–1942.* Iola, Wisconsin, 1985.

Lacey, Robert. *Ford: The Men and the Machine.* New York, 1986.

Langworth, Richard M. *Studebaker, 1946–1966.* Osceola, Wisconsin, 1979.

Langworth, Richard M. *The Last Onslaught on Detroit.* Princeton, New Jersey, 1975.

Leland, Ottilie M., and Mrs. Minnie Dubbs Millbrook. *Master of Precision.* Detroit, 1966.

Leslie, Stuart W. *Boss Kettering, Wizard of General Motors.* New York, 1983.

MacMinn, Strother, and Michael Lamm. *Detroit Style, Automotive Form 1925–1950.* Detroit, 1985.

Nesbitt, Dick. *50 Years of American Automobile Design.* Chicago, 1985.

Nevins, Allan, and Frank E. Hill. *Ford: Expansion and Challenge, 1915–1932.* New York, 1957.

Nevins, Allan, and Frank E. Hill. *Ford: Decline and Rebirth, 1933–1962.* New York, 1957.

Nevins, Allan, and Frank E. Hill. *Ford: The Times the Man and the Company.* New York, 1954.

Pound, Arthur. *The Turning Wheel: The Story of General Motors Through Twenty-Five Years, 1908–1933.* Garden City, New York, 1934

Rae, John B. *The American Automobile.* Chicago, 1965.

Riggs, L. Spencer. *Pace Cars of the Indy 500.* Ft. Lauderdale, Florida, 1989.

Sedgwick, Michael. *Cars of the 1930s.* Cambridge, Massachusetts, 1970.

Sedgwick, Michael. *Cars of the Thirties and Forties.* New York, 1979.

Sedgwick, Michael. *Cars of the 50s and 60s.* New York, 1983.

Turnquist, Robert E. *The Packard Story.* New York, 1965.

United States Government, Federal Trade Commission. *Report on Motor Vehicle Industry.* Washington, D.C., 1939.

Used Car Statistical Bureau. *Market Analysis Report.* Boston, 1941.

Ward, James A. *The Fall of the Packard Motor Car Company.* Stanford, California, 1995.

Weisberger, Bernard A. *The Dream Maker.* New York, 1979.

Wilkie, David J. and the editors of Esquire. *American Autos and Their Makers.* New York, 1963.

Young, Clarence H., and William A. Quinn. *Foundation for Living.* New York, 1963.

Index